Copyright © 2025 Brentwood Press

Scripture quotations marked NLT are taken from the Holy Bible, New Living Translation. © 1996, 2004, 2007, 2013 by Tyndale House Foundation. Used by permission of Tyndale House Publishers, Inc., Carol Stream, Illinois 60188. All rights reserved.

Scripture quotations marked NIV are taken from the Holy Bible, New International Version®, NIV®. Copyright © 1973, 1978, 1984, 2011 by Biblica, Inc.™ Used by permission of Zondervan. All rights reserved worldwide. www.zondervan.com. The "NIV" and "New International Version" are trademarks registered in the United States Patent and Trademark Office by Biblica, Inc.™

Scripture quotations marked NIRV are taken from the New International Reader's Version. Copyright © 1995, 1996, 1998, 2014 by Biblica, Inc.® Used by permission. All rights reserved worldwide.

Scripture quotations marked NASB are taken from the New American Standard Bible®, Copyright © 1960, 1962, 1963, 1968, 1971, 1972, 1973, 1975, 1977, 1995 by The Lockman Foundation. Used by permission. (www.Lockman.org)

Scripture quotations marked ICB are taken from the International Children's Bible®. Copyright © 1986, 1988, 1999 by Thomas Nelson. Used by permission. All rights reserved.

Scripture quotations marked HCSB are taken from the Holman Christian Standard Bible®, copyright © 1999, 2000, 2002, 2003, 2009 by Holman Bible Publishers. Used by permission. HCSB® is a federally registered trademarks of Holman Bible Publishers.

Scripture quotations marked NCV are taken from the New Century Version®. © 2005 by Thomas Nelson. Used by permission. All rights reserved.

Scripture quotations marked NKJV are taken from the New King James Version®. © 1982 by Thomas Nelson. Used by permission. All rights reserved.

Printed in China

First edition: 2025   10 9 8 7 6 5 4 3 2 1

Names: Humphrey, Sarah, author. | Thompson, Taylor, illustrator.

Title: 365 Family Devotional / written by Sarah Humphrey; illustrated by Taylor Thompson.

Description: Summary: Features 52 weeks of devotions to help families grow in their faith together and come face-to-face with God's endless love for them, providing a firm foundation of faith to last a lifetime. A companion to The Bible for Me: Bible Stories and Prayers.

Identifiers: ISBN: 978-1-57102-709-2

Subjects: LCSH Bible stories. | BISAC JUVENILE NONFICTION / Religion / Devotional Prayer

Classification: LCC BS551.2 .P372 2021 | DDC 220.9/505--dc23

Project management by Dan Lynch, Brentwood Press

Interior design by Diana Lawrence

Edited by Julie Monroe

Theological review by Doug Powell

Visit or contact us at TheBibleforMe.com

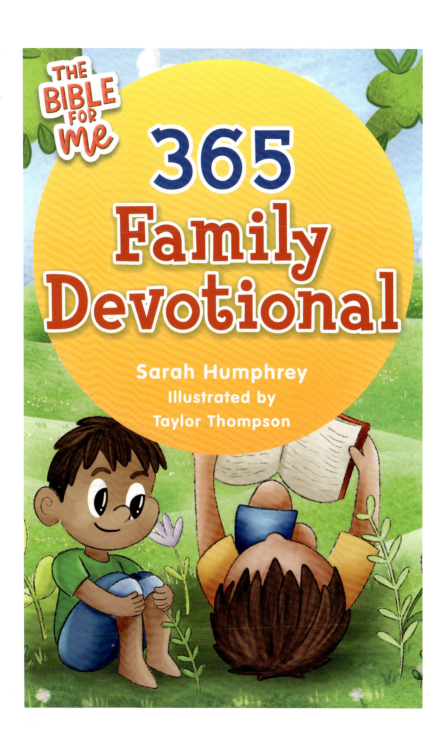

Dear Reader,

Thank you for bringing this *365 Family Devotional* to your table! We hope it encourages times of conversation and connection in your home, sheds light on important Biblical truths, and gives you fun opportunities to learn more about God's deep love for you!

365 Family Devotional, as part of *The Bible for Me*© series, was written to complement and enhance *The Bible Stories & Prayers Family Devotional*, as well as *Bible Stories & Prayers*, and *The Toddler Bible for Me*. At any time, you can reference the other books in *he Bible for Me*© series to customize each of these stories to the specific age ranges of your children. The *365 Family Devotional* takes one year to complete, travels through the most known stories of the Bible one week at a time and is divided into small devotions and activities for young families.

The best way to use this devotional is to take note of the simple, weekly pattern for each Bible Story presentation. Every seven days, a new story is presented with Scripture

references, along with a short summary. On the six days following the weekly reading and story, you will be led through a day of prayer focus, a day to concentrate on memorizing the Scripture verse of the week, a day set aside for short activities, a day dedicated to talk as a family, a day to accomplish some simple act of service, and finally, a family time set aside to cook or snack on an easy recipe. If you are using this devotional as part of a homeschool curriculum, it might be helpful to glance at each week ahead of time. Very few uncommon materials are suggested; but knowing ahead of time of the need for any additional supplies can certainly be helpful.

Enjoy these times of encountering Scripture and connection, and relish in how much God cares for you and your family!

In His Love, Sarah

Old Testament Bible Story Devotions

Week 1....The Very Beginning (Genesis 1–2) 8
Week 2....Adam and Eve Mess Up (Genesis 2–3) 15
Week 3....God Starts Over (Genesis 6–9) 22
Week 4....God's Promise to Abraham (Genesis 12–13, 15, 17–18, 21) 29
Week 5....Abraham Gives His Best (Genesis 22) 36
Week 6....Jacob's and Esau's Blessings (Genesis 24–25, 27) 43
Week 7....Joseph Helps His Brothers (Genesis 37, 39–45) 50
Week 8....Baby Moses Is Saved (Exodus 1–2) 57
Week 9....God Calls Moses (Exodus 2–4) 64
Week 10...God Splits the Red Sea (Exodus 4–15) 71
Week 11...Moses on the Mountain (Exodus 19–20) 78
Week 12...Exploring Canaan (Numbers 13–14) 85
Week 13...Joshua and the Big Wall (Joshua 6) 92
Week 14...Gideon and the Tiny Army (Judges 6–7) 99
Week 15...God Calls Samuel (1 Samuel 1–3) 106
Week 16...David Fights a Giant (1 Samuel 17) 113
Week 17...Jonathan Helps His Best Friend (1 Samuel 18, 20) 120
Week 18...A King After God's Own Heart (1 Samuel 16; 2 Samuel 2) 127
Week 19...The Wise King (1 Kings 3) 134
Week 20...The One True God (1 Kings 18) 141
Week 21...Elisha, the Prophet's Apprentice (1 Kings 19; 2 Kings 2, 4) 148
Week 22...The Girl Who Saved Her People (Esther 1–10) 155
Week 23...Three Friends in the Hot Seat (Daniel 3) 162
Week 24...Daniel and the Friendly Lions (Daniel 6) 169
Week 25...Jonah and the Great Fish (Jonah 1–4) 176

New Testament Bible Story Devotions

Week 26..Gabriel Visits Mary and Joseph (Luke 1:26–38; Matthew 1:18–25)...........183
Week 27...God with Us (Matthew 1:25; Luke 2:1–20)...............................190
Week 28..Wise Men Worship Jesus (Matthew 2:1–12)................................197
Week 29..Jesus in His Father's House (Luke 2:41–50)............................ 204
Week 30..Jesus Is Baptized (Luke 1; Matthew 3; John 1)......................... 211
Week 31..Jesus Stands Up to Evil (Matthew 4:1–11)...............................218
Week 32. The Disciples Follow Jesus (Luke 5:1–11, 27–28; 6:12–16;
          Matthew 9:9; John 1:35–50)... 225
Week 33..One Man Thanks Jesus (Luke 17:11–19).................................. 232
Week 34..The Sermon on the Mount (Matthew 5–7)................................. 239
Week 35..Jesus Feeds Five Thousand (John 6:1–14)............................... 246
Week 36..Above the Waves (Matthew 14:22–33; Mark 6:45–52; John 6:16–21)........ 253
Week 37..Who Is Your Neighbor? (Luke 10:25–37)................................. 260
Week 38..Sibling Rivalry (Luke 10:38–42) 267
Week 39. The Wind and the Waves Obey Him (Matthew 8:23–27; Mark 4:35–41;
          Luke 8:22–25) 274
Week 40..The Great Healer (Matthew 9:18–26; Mark 5:21–43; Luke 8:40–56).........281
Week 41..Let Them Come! (Matthew 19:14; Mark 10:13–15) 288
Week 42..The Widow's Offering (Mark 12:38–44; Luke 21:1–4) 295
Week 43..The Lamb of God (Matt. 26:17–29; Mark 14:12–25; Luke 22:7–20; John 13:1–20). 302
Week 44. A Lonely Night in the Garden (Matthew 26:30, 36–56; Mark 14:26, 32–52;
          Luke 22:39–53; John 18:1–12)... 309
Week 45..Jesus Dies (Matthew 27; Mark 15; Luke 22:66–71; John 18:28–19:42).....316
Week 46..Jesus Is Alive! (Matthew 28:1–15; Mark 16:1–12; Luke 24; John 20)..... 323
Week 47..The Good News (Matthew 28:16–20)...................................... 330
Week 48..Jesus Goes to Heaven (Luke 24; Acts 1)................................ 337
Week 49..The Disciples Spread the Word (Acts 2–3, 9, 12, 16) 344
Week 50..John Sees Heaven (Revelation 1, 4, 21).................................351
Week 51..The Old Testament 368
Week 52 .The New Testament... 375

The Very Beginning
Genesis 1-2

Do you know how everything started? Before there were any of us, even before there was an earth, all was dark. Scripture tells us "the earth was formless and empty" and "darkness was over the surface of the deep" (Genesis 1:2; NIV). Then God spoke into the emptiness, light appeared and changed everything. In six days, God created day and night, dry land, plants and trees, and the sun, moon, and stars. Then He made birds in the sky, land and sea animals of all sizes, and even man and woman. Each day, after creating, He smiled and said: "It is good." On the seventh day, God was finished with creation, so He blessed the day and made it holy.

It's fascinating to think about how God created everything. God made each of us with intentionality and a purpose. God has unlimited creativity and power. Of all that He could have created, He chose to make each one of us. Imagine how much He must love us! We are God's workmanship and also His children.

God, thank You for creating the heavens, the earth, and each one of us. Help us to learn how to hear Your voice and love You in return. Amen.

January 2

A Simple Prayer

This month, we are celebrating God's creativity and the devoted love He showed in making the world and in making us! When we take the time to reflect on His devotion to us, it helps us build a strong foundation and grasp His purpose for His people. By learning about God's intentions and His heart for us, we can receive and be fulfilled by all that He has for us. As we learn, we can share His love with others.

During January, pray this simple prayer with your family, thanking God for His devotion to you!

Jesus, Thank You for Your devotion to us. Help us to be devoted to You! Teach us how to cultivate devotion in our lives and in our relationships with one another. Help us to grow and serve You always. Amen.

January 3

Bible Verse of the Week

"God saw all that he had made, and it was very good."
—Genesis 1:31 NIV

This week, we learned about how God made the heavens, Earth, and all people and animals. What an amazing Creator! After each day's creative work, God looked at what He had created and called it good.

One of the best ways to grow personally and as a family is to memorize Scripture.

Take the time this week to memorize Genesis 1:31 with your family! Write it out and post it to your refrigerator. Let everyone in your family have the opportunity to say it aloud, then say it all together. Have fun enjoying the Word of God as a family!

God, thank You for the Bible. Help us to memorize Your Word and to hide it in our hearts. Amen.

January 4

Do It!

It's time time to make the story of creation feel real! Take the opportunity to go outside and look around at all that God created. Do you see the skies, trees, and sunshine? Is the temperature cool or comfortable? Are there animals around? All of these are tangible signs of God's creation right in front of you.

Pick up a piece of dirt, or perhaps a pile of snow. Look at it closely, feel it, and smell it. God made each of these things and called them good. Not only did He make the world and everything in it, He also intentionally made you and your family.

God, thank You for making the world and everything in it. Open our eyes to see Your creation each day. Amen.

January 5

Talk About It!

This week, you've learned about the creation story as a family. You spent time praying, memorizing Scripture, and taking some time outside in nature. What was your favorite activity together? Why?

We've discussed and experienced many things this week regarding creation and family. With all that in mind, here is a question to chat about together: If you could create anything, what would it be? Spend some time together as a family talking about your week and sharing about what you might like to create to make this world a better and brighter place.

Thank God for all that He created, including you and your family.

Dear God, help us be creative as You are. Give us ideas for new and wonderful solutions to make this world a better place. Amen.

January 6

Serve One Another

Any time we read Scripture, it gives us an opportunity to love and serve one another. Think about the verse and prayer you are memorizing this week:

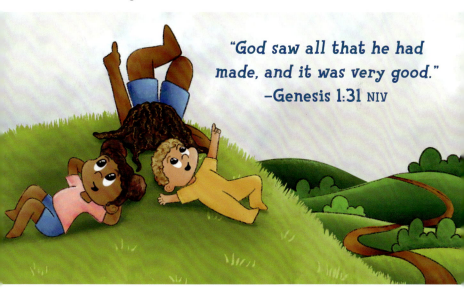

"God saw all that he had made, and it was very good."
–Genesis 1:31 NIV

Let's put God's love in action by intentionally affirming each other. Think about each person in your family. Take time today to write a note or tell a family member that you truly see them and love them. Tell them a few things that you enjoy about them, share a funny memory or two, and let them know that you care about them. It's always a good idea to tell the ones we are closest to how much we appreciate and love them!

God, Thank You for each person in our family. Thank You for creating each one of us and calling us good. Amen.

January 7

Eat Together

Time for a recipe! Cooking and working with food are fun ways to express our God-given creativity. Grab these ingredients for a charcuterie board and enjoy a treat as a family.

Head to the store and stock up on some favorite snacks. Some ideas include grapes, strawberries, blueberries, cheese blocks, pretzels, crackers, cherry tomatoes, and carrot sticks. Design a family charcuterie board to snack on while you sit at the table and share about this week's lesson and your time together. Your family is made in His image, and You are good.

God, thank You for time devoted to You as a family this week. Help us continue to learn together and share time in Your Word. We are thankful for You. Amen.

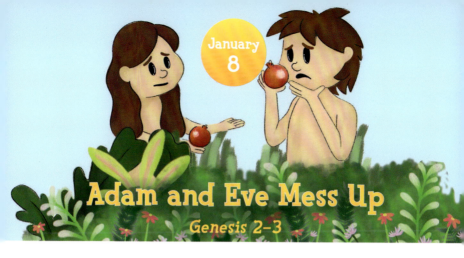

Adam and Eve Mess Up
Genesis 2–3

God created each of us; He loves us unconditionally in the midst of our imperfect lives! Adam and Eve learned this early on. After God created Adam, he put him in a beautiful garden and gave him one instruction: Enjoy it all; but do not eat from the Tree of the Knowledge of Good and Evil."

You would think one rule would be simple enough to follow, right? Unfortunately, it was not. Eve was tricked by the sneaky serpent to eat fruit from the tree. Then she fed some to Adam. As soon as they ate, they felt ashamed. They knew they had done wrong, and they hid from God. God knew what had happened and called out to them. He still loved them but had to discipline them and punish the snake for their sinful actions.

Though God continued to care for them, Adam and Eve had to live a very different lives than the perfect ones God had originally provided for them. Such is the case with all of us.

God, thank You for providing for us, even when we mess up. Help us to learn about Your grace (unmerited favor) and mercy (kindness and forgiveness) from Adam and Eve's story.

January 9

A Simple Prayer

This month, we are celebrating God's creativity and the devoted love He displayed in making the world and in making us! When God made Adam and Eve, He had wonderful intentions for them to live in close fellowship with Him inside the perfect Garden of Eden. When they messed up, there were consequences. Yet even in those consequences, God's love for them was unchanging. As we take the time to reflect on God's unwavering devotion to us, let's continue to pray this month's prayer as a family, thanking God for His devotion to all of us!

Jesus, thank You for Your devotion to us. Help us to be devoted to You! Teach us how to cultivate devotion in our lives and in our relationships with one another. Help us to grow and serve You always. Amen.

January 10

Bible Verse of the Week

"Then the LORD God called to the man, Where are you?'"
–Genesis 3:9 NLT

T his week, we learned how Adam and Eve disobeyed. We also learned about God's care and the consequences they faced in the midst of their shame.

One of the best ways to grow personally and as a family is to memorize Scripture. As we encounter both love and discipline this week, take the time to memorize Genesis 3:9 with your family! Write it out and post it to your refrigerator. Let everyone in your family have the opportunity to say it aloud, and then say it all together. Have fun enjoying the Word of God as a family!

God, thank You for the Bible. Help us to memorize Your Word and to hide it in our hearts. Amen.

January 11

Do It!

This week's story can feel a little like a game of hide and seek with God. When Adam and Eve knew they had done wrong, they hid from Him in shame. God called out to them, knowing they were embarrassed and were nervous to see Him. Have you ever hid from someone or something when you knew you did wrong?

Take some time and play a game of hide and seek in your home. While you are enjoying the fun of being together and finding good spots to tuck away into, remember the story of Adam and Eve. Remember that even though they did wrong, God still called out for them. He loved them in the midst of their embarrassment, and He set them on a new path.

God, Thank You for loving us even when we are ashamed, embarrassed, and scared. Help us to talk to You when we mess up. Amen.

Talk About It!

Have you ever done something wrong? Of course you have. We all have! Ever since Adam and Eve messed up, we have all been messing up. The good news is that Jesus came to save us from the consequences of our sin. Our job is to recognize it when we sin, say we are sorry, and ask for God's forgiveness. When we do that, He will forgive us and give us the strength to do better the next time.

It's common to feel ashamed or embarrassed when we do wrong, but God is faithful to us! We don't have to be nervous or scared to talk to Him about it. He wants us to come to Him when we do wrong and are disobedient, even when what we've done is really bad. Nothing can separate us from His love. We just need to go to Him with faith and repentance.

God, thank You for being the perfect Father. Help us to remember to come to You with our struggles, disobedience, and obedience! Amen.

January 13

Serve One Another

One of the primary ways God develops family life is through honesty. Sometimes, we can feel shame when we do what is wrong, just like Adam and Eve. Yet having a family we can turn to for confession and support can be just the thing that helps our hearts and our behavior transform.

Take the time this week to serve one another in your family by confessing any struggle you may be having. By being honest with each other and living in God's light, we support one another with the love of Jesus. Pray for your family members this week while you face your own struggle. Know that you are loved!

God, thank You for the love of a caring family. Help us to confess to one another and support each other. Amen.

January 14

Eat Together

What's your favorite type of food that involves an apple? Even though we don't know what fruit Eve ate from The Tree of the Knowledge of Good and Evil, it may have been an apple; and apples are truly a good snack! Consider a trip to the grocery store or farmer's market to grab a few different kinds of apples (Fuji, Green, Honey Crisp, etc.); you may even choose dried apples or applesauce. Enjoy the flavors—the similarities and differences of each type. If you're up for it, you can even bake an apple pie.

Whatever you decide, give thanks to God for His creation. And enjoy the sweetness!

God, thank You for the delicious foods of the Earth. Help us to remember to give thanks when we eat and to let you guide our life choices! Amen.

January 15

God Starts Over
Genesis 6–9

Many years passed after Adam and Eve, and people still made bad decisions and disobeyed God. There was only one man, named Noah, who obeyed God. "God was sad about everything happening on Earth and he told Noah that He was going to cause rain to flood the land and wash away evil. God wanted to save Noah, his family, and the animals. So, God instructed Noah to build a giant boat (called an ark) for when the rain arrived. Even though it may have seemed crazy, Noah did what God said. He was to build a massive boat from cypress wood, waterproof it, and make stalls for the animals inside (Genesis 6:14–15; NLT).

When the rain came, he, his family, and the animals were safe. After many months, Noah checked to see if the land was finally dry by sending a dove out of the ark. When the dove came back with an olive leaf, Noah knew that it was finally time to leave the ark and start over again.

Dear God, thank You for instructing and guiding us, even if we don't understand at the time. Help us to trust You in all situations. Amen.

A Simple Prayer

This month we are celebrating God's creativity and the devoted love He showed in making the world and in making us! Just like Noah, we can be sure that trusting and obeying God is always the right thing to do. Because God's intentions and His heart for us is good, we obey what He asks, even if it is hard to understand at the time. When we trust and believe God, we can share that faith with others.

During January, pray this simple prayer with your family, thanking God for His devotion to you!

Jesus, thank You for Your devotion to us. Help us to be devoted to You! Teach us how to cultivate devotion in our lives and in our relationships with one another. Help us to grow and serve You always. Amen.

Bible Verse of the Week

"So Noah did everything exactly as God had commanded him."
–Genesis 6:22 NLT

We learned this week how Noah obeyed God. We discovered that God values our obedience to Him because His ways are good. One of the best ways to grow personally and as a family is to memorize Scripture. As we begin to understand both love and obedience this week, take the time to memorize Genesis 6:22 with your family! Write it out and post it to your refrigerator. Let everyone in your family have the opportunity to say it aloud, and then say it all together. Have fun enjoying the Word of God as a family!

God, thank You for the Bible. Help us to memorize Your Word and to hide it in our hearts. Amen.

Do It!

Not only was Noah responsible for taking care of his family on the ark, but God also asked him to care for the animals. Do you care for a pet or animal? Maybe you have a dog, cat, turtle, or even a chicken, horse, or cow. If you do, you know that pets are a wonderful part of life. Some can provide us with important resources like milk or eggs; nearly all of them are fun to be around. Taking care of our pets well is a way we can honor and obey God. If you have a pet, consider being in charge of feeding it this week. Maybe ask if you can take your pet on a walk. If your home or barn is suitable, perhaps you could even bathe it! Celebrate God's care for animals by loving on a pet this week.

Dear God, thank You for our pets and for animals. Help us to care for our furry and feathered friends in the ways You have intended. Amen.

Talk About It

Hopefully you had the opportunity to love on an animal this week, either your own or a friend's. If you don't have an animal to care for, take a few minutes to talk or dream with your family about it! Maybe getting a real pet is a possibility, but perhaps it's not. Either way, you can talk about what animals you love or would enjoy caring for.

You can also imagine which animals would be a hilarious addition to your home. What would it be like to host an elephant in the living room? What if you decided to keep an ostrich in the backyard? What would you have to do care for all the animals if your house was the ark?

Laugh and enjoy the time together, sharing in both God's love for animals and His humor.

Dear God, thank You for the animals on the Earth. And thank You for not having to keep all of them in our house! Amen.

January 20

Serve One Another

We've taken the time to serve and care for animals this week, but what about serving your family? Living on a boat for months with only family members, as Noah did, might be a little rough. Thankfully, this isn't the case for you right now. Still, you may have to share a room with a sibling or wait for a turn in the bathroom. You may have to do everyone's dishes after dinner.

Whether our families live on a boat, in a house or in an apartment, we still need to take care of our space and be considerate of one another. Think of a way you can help around your home this week. Things as simple as putting your shoes away or putting your dirty bowl in the dishwasher may seem small; but doing your part is a big deal, especially to your mom and dad.

Dear God, thank You that we are able to serve our family and our home. Help us to remember to be quick to clean up after ourselves. Amen.

Eat Together

It's snack time! Grab a bag of animal crackers, peanut butter or Nutella™, a banana or two, and a knife.

Place the banana on a plate in front of you and cut it in half longwise. Dip your knife in the peanut butter or Nutella™ and spread it across the banana. Grab whatever animal crackers you like and stand them up along the center of the banana. When your creation looks like animals in a boat, take a selfie or photos with your food art, and enjoy your treat!

Dear God, thank You for constant reminders of Your faithfulness—from the food You grow on Earth to the animal crackers we can buy from the store. Help us to be grateful for what we have and to remember Your instructions in everything we do. Amen.

January 22

God's Promise to Abraham

Genesis 12–13, 15, 17–18, 21

More than 300 years after Noah, Abram was on the scene. The Lord called to him and said "Go from your country, your people and your father's household to the land I will show you (Genesis 12:1; NIV)." Abram didn't know all about what that meant, but he knew God promised to show him the way. God showed him the stars in the sky and told Abram to count them because he would someday have as many descendants as there were stars. Abram was old at the time, and his wife, Sarai, was well past the age to be a mom. Sarai overheard God say their new names were to be Abraham and Sarah and that she would have a son named Isaac by the same time the following year. Abraham wondered how this could be, and Sarah even laughed in disbelief, as her age seemed to make that impossible. But the Lord confronted them saying: "Is there anything I can't do?"

One year later, Isaac was born. Nothing is too hard for the Lord.

Dear God, thank You for your faithfulness even when we struggle to believe You. Always remind us that nothing is too hard for You. Amen.

A Simple Prayer

This month, we are celebrating God's creativity and the devoted love He showed in making the world and in making us! As we learn about the story of Abraham and Sarah, we can be sure that God keeps His promises, even if they seem impossible. By listening to God's intentions and His heart for us, we can receive all that He has for us in such a fulfilling way. Abraham and Sarah surely did!

During January, pray this simple prayer with your family, thanking God for His devotion to you!

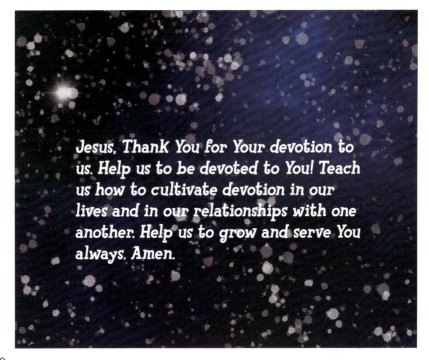

Jesus, Thank You for Your devotion to us. Help us to be devoted to You! Teach us how to cultivate devotion in our lives and in our relationships with one another. Help us to grow and serve You always. Amen.

Bible Verse of the Week

"Is anything too difficult for the LORD?"
(Genesis 18:14; NASB)

One of the best ways to grow personally, and as a family, is to memorize Scripture.

This week, we learned how Abraham and Sarah received God's promise. We discovered that God wants us to trust Him because nothing is too hard for the Lord.

As you understand more about love and trust this week, take the time to memorize Genesis 18:14 with your family! Write it out and post it to your refrigerator. Let each person in your family have the opportunity to say it aloud, and then say it all together. Have fun enjoying the Word of God as a family!

Dear God, thank You for the Bible. Help us to memorize Your Word and to hide it in our hearts. Amen.

January 25
Do It!

We've been spending time in Genesis the last few weeks. It is a book with a lot of promises. All of Scripture is full of promises, and there is much to explore! Grab your Bible and look through it for your favorite promise from God. If you need help, you can grab a concordance or Google "Bible promises." When you find the verse that speaks to you the most, write it out with color and doodles. Share it with your family; then frame it or hang it in a special place in your room where you will see it often. If you have a phone, you can even take a photo of it and set it as your background. Go back to it whenever you need a reminder that God sees you and provides for you.

Dear God, thank You for your promises to us. Help us to trust You, to remember Your Word, and to be encouraged by You. Amen.

Talk About It

Think about a time when you felt like a circumstance was impossible. What was it and what did you do about it? Did you confront the situation, or try to make something happen on your own? Did you ignore the problem and just give up? Chat about this topic with your family around the dinner table. Listen to the stories of others and share your own.

With each situation that is shared, ask "What did you learn from your circumstance?" "Did it end up ok, or did it end up in shambles?" Now that you know the story of Abraham and Sarah, how might their actions impact your choices in the future? Talk it over and spend a few minutes in prayer, asking God to increase your trust in Him!

Dear God, help us to trust You in all things, even if they seem impossible. Please give us Your strength and the tools we need to be part of what You are doing on the Earth. Amen.

Serve One Another

Sometimes, believing God means taking action, even if we don't feel like it. Take action this week! If you are procrastinating on a project, get started. Maybe you can clean out the garage or the family car. Perhaps you can re-organize the pantry or even start an exercise or healthy meal plan for the family.

When life or certain projects seem overwhelming, just remember to take the first step! God is with you in the process, and nothing is too hard for Him. If you get started, He is sure to be with You in your obedience. Make sure, though, to keep a good attitude and perhaps get yourself a small treat after you accomplish your goal!

Dear God, thank You for motivating us with Your Spirit. Help us to move toward You by taking action on Your instructions. Amen.

January 28

Eat Together

Let's get snacking! You'll need two slices of bread per person, peanut butter and jelly (or spreads of your choice), and a knife.

Pass out two pieces of bread to each person. Give a knife to each so they can spread the peanut butter and jelly (or whatever you've chosen) over the bread. Close the bread together. Each person should try to cut their sandwich into a star shape. Some stars may look more star-like than others, and that is ok! Have fun with the process.

Enjoy your sandwiches while remembering that God promised Abraham he would have as many descendants as there are stars in the sky! God did exactly that for Abraham. He will fulfill His promises to You, too.

Dear God, thank You for food to eat and promises fulfilled. Help us to be grateful as we wait for You. Amen.

Abraham Gives His Best
Genesis 22

January 29

When Abraham's son, Isaac, grew to be a young boy, the Lord told Abraham to take Isaac to the mountains and offer him as a sacrifice. Abraham saddled his donkey, gathered what they needed, and did as God asked. When they arrived at the place where God led them, Abraham prepared the altar where Isaac was to be sacrificed.

Knowing that Isaac was his promise from God, Abraham still moved forward with the instructions. Isaac even asked questions about what they would sacrifice when they arrived, and Abraham kept reminding his son that the Lord would provide. Just as Abraham was about to fulfill God's request, the Lord stopped him. God didn't want him to follow through, He simply wanted to know that Abraham loved Him even more than he loved Isaac. Abraham looked up and saw a ram caught in the bushes nearby. He sacrificed the ram to the Lord instead of Isaac. The Lord provided.

Dear God, thank You for Your care and provision. Help us to obey You even when we don't want to, knowing that Your ways are bigger than we can understand. Amen.

A Simple Prayer

This month we are celebrating God's creativity and the devoted love He showed in making the world and in making us!

Abraham trusted God, even when faced with the most impossibly difficult task. Because he responded to God with the same devotion God has for us, the Lord was gracious to save Isaac. God's intentions and His heart toward us are good, even when we don't fully understand. We can trust Him and follow through with whatever He requests of us. When we do, we will see His provision for us more clearly.

During January, pray this simple prayer with your family, thanking God for His devotion to you!

Jesus, thank You for Your devotion to us. Help us to be devoted to You! Teach us how to cultivate devotion in our lives and in our relationships with one another. Help us to grow and serve You always. Amen.

Bible Verse of the Week

"The lord says, 'Because you did not keep back your son, your only son, from me, I make you this promise by my own name: I will surely bless you and give you many descendants'" (Genesis 22:16-1;7 NCV).

One of the best ways to grow personally, and as a family, is to memorize Scripture.

This week, we learned how Abraham trusted God. We discovered that God values our trust in Him because He is devoted to us.

As you grow in both faith and obedience this week, take the time to memorize Genesis 22:16–17 with your family! Write it out and post it to your refrigerator. Let each person in your family have the opportunity to say it aloud, and then say it all together. Have fun enjoying the Word of God as a family!

God, thank You for the Bible. Help us to memorize Your Word and to hide it in our hearts. Amen.

Do it!

Sometimes we can get careless, complacent, or selfish instead of giving God our best efforts. Abraham's devotion and commitment were tested by God. When God asked Abraham to sacrifice his only son, the son who was promised, he was likely startled. Abraham must have had to think over whether or not he really wanted to give back to God the most precious gift God had given him. Yet Abraham trusted God, even though he didn't understand. And because of that trust and the decision to give God his best, the Lord saved Isaac. It was only a test!

Think about how many times you are tempted to withhold from God the very best you have to offer. It could be often. Consider how you can give back to Him in the devoted ways He has given to you. Perhaps spend intentional time in prayer today, help a brother or sibling out, or give away a bit of your money to someone in need. Whatever you choose to do, give the Lord your best, knowing that He will provide for you!

Dear God, thank You for giving us Your best! Help us to be devoted to You and give back to You with our best efforts, as well. Amen.

Talk About It

Spend some time with your family around the table this week and consider the ways you can give back to God. What do you like to do? Maybe you enjoy sports or reading or cooking. Whatever you enjoy doing, you can do it all for the glory of God. By working hard and being devoted to healthy discipline, you can let your light shine and help others see God's good fruit in you!

Talk with your family and help each other see the good in one another. Encourage each other to be the best they can be through their gifts, talents, and character. Be strengthened and challenged by seeing the best in others. Recognize your own gifts and then give them back to God by showing Him proper gratitude and giving Him credit.

Dear God, You are the best, and Your light heals us. Help us to encourage one another and challenge each other to give back to You with our gifts, talent, and character. Amen.

Serve One Another

This week, we have been talking about God's devotion to us and our devotion to Him. Spend today considering the good gifts God has given you. What promises has God fulfilled for you? Write an encouraging note to someone who may be struggling. When you realize that the Lord has provided for you, you can help strengthen the faith of someone who needs to trust God through a hard season.

Consider how Abraham must have felt when God directed him to walk all the way up the mountain, dreading what waited at the top. Remind your friend that God cares for him or her and will provide what is needed! Everyone can use a kind word during times of testing.

Dear God, bless my friends with trust and faith in You. Help me be encouraging to others when they are tested and their faith grows dim. Amen.

Eat Together

Time for some chili! Spend today chatting and chopping while discussing all you learned about Abraham's big test. Once your efforts are complete, enjoy a bowl together, and celebrate God's faithfulness!

You'll need:
2 pounds ground beef or turkey
½ onion
1 green pepper
1 stalk of celery
1 can light kidney beans
1 can black beans
1 can corn
1 large can diced tomatoes
1 large can stewed tomatoes
1 packet chili seasoning

Toppings (optional):
Sour cream, shredded cheese, avocado, crackers

Sauté ground beef or turkey on the stovetop until done. Chop/dice raw veggies. Transfer cooked beef/turkey to a crock pot. Add prepared veggies. Pour in beans, corn, tomatoes, and seasoning. Let the mixture cook for about 4 hours. Pour into bowls, and finish off with your favorite toppings.

February 5

Jacob's and Esau's Blessings
Genesis 24–25, 27

When Abraham's son, Isaac, grew up, he married a woman named Rebekah. She became pregnant with twins. While she was pregnant, she could feel them wrestling in her belly. God spoke to her and said she would have two boys. The older son, Esau, would serve the younger one, Jacob. This was contrary to custom, as the oldest son was the heir to all the father possessed and the recipient of his blessing. When the boys grew older, Jacob stayed home close to his mother, and Esau spent time hunting in the untamed areas surrounding their home.

One day, Jacob came in from the fields and was very hungry, so he made a pot of soup. Esau asked if he could have some. Jacob replied: "I will only give you soup if you give me your birthright!" Esau was so desperately hungry that he complied. Not long afterward, Isaac was old and dying; he sent Esau to hunt for game to make one last meal, after which, Isaac would bless Esau. Isaac's eyesight was weak, so while Esau was gone, Jacob dressed as Esau to trick Isaac into giving him the blessing instead. Though Esau still received a blessing, Jacob became his father's heir. The older son served the younger, just as God had said.

Dear God, thank You for blessing the siblings in our household. Help us to be kind and patient, while allowing each other to receive from You. Amen.

A Simple Prayer

This month we are celebrating God's love for His children! As we continue to learn the story of Jacob and Esau, we can be sure that God loves all His children, even if they argue and challenge one another. By receiving God's blessings and His care for us, we can grow into the men and women God has created us to be and be fulfilled by living out His plan for our lives.

During February, pray this simple prayer with your family, thanking God for His love for you!

Jesus, You are love. Thank You for loving us unconditionally, when we do well and when we fail. Your love for us saves us. Teach us how to cultivate love in our lives and in our relationships with one another. Help us to grow and serve you always. Amen.

Bible Verse of the Week

"The LORD told her, 'The sons in your womb will become two nations . . . one nation will be stronger than the other; and your older son will serve your younger son' (Genesis 25:23; NLT).

One of the best ways to grow personally and as a family is to memorize Scripture.

This week, we learned how Jacob and Esau received God's blessing from their father. We discovered that God wants us to trust Him with our futures.

As you consider both sibling rivalry and trust this week, take the time to memorize Genesis 25:23 with your family! Write it out and post it to your refrigerator. Let each person in your family have the opportunity to say it aloud, and then say it all together. Have fun enjoying the Word of God as a family!

Dear God, thank You for the Bible. Help us to memorize Your Word and to hide it in our hearts. Amen.

February 8

Do it!

Have you ever had a goal or dream that you really wanted to come true? Just as Jacob and Esau both wanted their father's blessing, we want to receive God's blessing on our lives. Sit at the table with your family and take turns talking about personal hopes and dreams. What practical steps do each of you need to take in order to do what you would like to do? Say a prayer about the desires in each heart and ask God to be with each of you every step of the way. Be open to the fact that things may change as you go through life but know that God always has your best interests at heart! His blessing is our best confirmation.

Dear God, thank You for blessing us with hopes and dreams. Please help us commit those hopes and dreams to You. Lead us in every way we go. Amen.

February 9

Talk About It

When you read the story about Jacob and Esau, what do you think about the tradeoff that happened? Do you relate more to Jacob or to Esau? Have you ever passed up a good thing to meet a temporary need or want? Did that work out for you or not?

Jacob and Esau wrestled even in the womb, and it was clear that they were very different in appearance and personality when they were born. If you have siblings in your family, you might very well understand how those relationships can be both a blessing and a challenge. Jacob and Esau show us that the people in the Bible were human beings who made mistakes and wrong decisions. It's a good thing God loves us deeply and cares for us, even when we choose to be selfish! We should be so grateful for His grace over us!

Dear God, I am sorry for the times I have been selfish or have chosen to do the wrong thing, especially on purpose. Please help me make wise choices. Amen.

Serve One Another

This week, we learned about one sibling taking the blessing from the other. But what if you could give blessings instead of competing for them? Take this opportunity, as you sit together around the table, to take turns blessing each person in your family. Maybe this means saying a prayer for each person, or giving a word of encouragement to all, or even helping set the table.

There are simple ways that you can practice sharing blessings every single day, especially in the context of family. You can bless your mom by making her a cup of coffee; you can bless your dad by turning off the lights when you leave a room! You can make sure to replace the toilet paper roll when needed, or make sure your socks are not inside out when they go into the washing machine (moms will get it!). Whatever you do, do it to bless those in your family.

Dear God, please remind me that little acts of service go a long way. Help me to bless those around me with my words and actions. Amen.

Eat Together

Just like Esau came home exhausted from a long hunting trip, you are probably tired after a busy week. Soup was a great meal for him then and a great one for you now. Think simply this week by grabbing a few cans or boxes of your favorite soup from the store. Chop up a few additional vegetables that will make your soup fresh and filling. Set aside a loaf of your favorite bread and butter.

Heat your soup on the stove or in a crock pot and place your bread in a warm oven for a few minutes. Enjoy your meal without the fear of losing your blessing. Instead, pray over your simple meal, and thank God for blessing you with a wonderfully full belly.

Dear God, please bless our meal, whether we make it from scratch or buy it from the store. Help us to be grateful for our food, and let it nourish our bodies to serve You better. Amen.

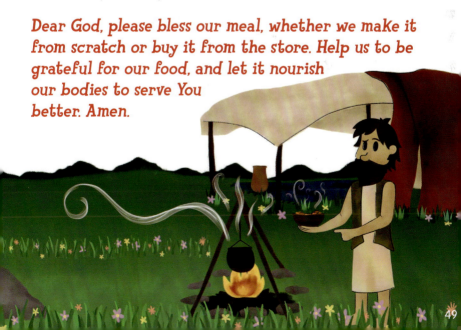

February 12

Joseph Helps His Brothers
Genesis 37, 39–45

Jacob, Abraham's youngest son and heir, went on to have twelve sons, and his favorite one was Joseph. Jacob gave Joseph a colorful robe as a special gift, and his brothers didn't like that very much. Joseph also had dreams of having his brothers bow down to him, and they really didn't like that! Because they were jealous, they took Joseph's robe and threw him into a pit. Eventually, they sold him to some traders and tried to tell their dad that a wild animal ate him. Joseph ended up in jail in Egypt, but God was with him. He interpreted dreams for the people in jail, and the king heard about it.

The king had a dream and called Joseph to interpret it; Joseph understood the dream was a warning that a famine was coming. The king put Joseph in charge of storing up grain, so they would be ready. After the famine hit, Joseph's brothers were running out of food and were sent to the king's palace to get some. Little did they know, Joseph was in charge. Joseph ended up forgiving his brothers and helping them, even though they tried to hurt him.

Dear God, thank You for watching over us, even when others try to hurt us. Help us to remember that You turn all things for good. Amen.

A Simple Prayer

This month we are celebrating God's love for His children!

We learn from the story of Joseph that God gave him a heart of love and forgiveness, even though his brothers tried to get him killed. By accepting difficult times and looking for God's mercy within them, we can be fulfilled by becoming all He has made us to be.

During February, pray this simple prayer with your family, thanking God for His love for you!

Jesus, You are love. Thank You for loving us unconditionally when we do well and when we fail. Your love for us saves us. Teach us how to cultivate love in our lives and in our relationships with one another. Help us to grow and serve you always. Amen.

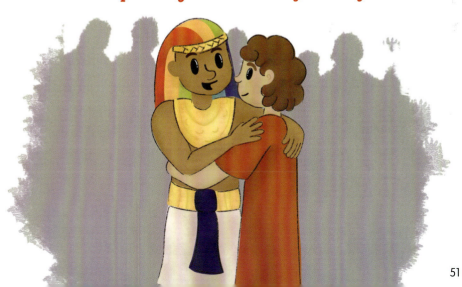

Bible Verse of the Week

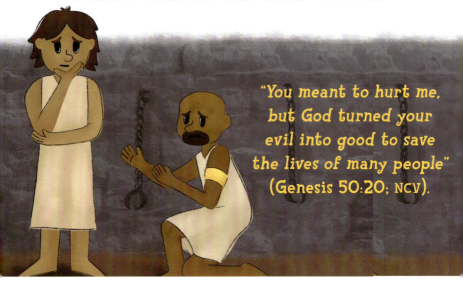

"You meant to hurt me, but God turned your evil into good to save the lives of many people" (Genesis 50:20; NCV).

One of the best ways to grow personally, and as a family, is to memorize Scripture.

This week, we learned how Joseph received God's blessing even when he was betrayed by his brothers. We discovered that God wants us to trust Him even when we are hurt and wronged.

As you examine both sibling rivalry and God's faithfulness this week, take the time to memorize Genesis 50:20 with your family! Write it out and post it to your refrigerator. Let each person in your family have the opportunity to say it aloud, and then say it all together. Have fun enjoying the Word of God as a family!

Dear God, thank You for the Bible. Help us to memorize Your Word and to hide it in our hearts. Amen.

Do it!

We all know there are some difficult things happening in the world right now. Sit down with your family and make a list of some things that are troubling. Talk to God together about each one of these situations and ask God to do what He did for Joseph—turn the bad things to good. Ask Him to help your family be an example of love and forgiveness for the world around you.

Anytime you feel ungrateful for the life you have, go back to this list of difficult world situations and remember that many people need Jesus. You can cultivate gratitude in your daily life by praying for those around you who are experiencing hard circumstances.

Dear God, thank You for turning awful things to good. We know you are able and we can be faithful to pray and help in the ways you lead us. Give us Your heart for the world around us. Amen.

February 16
Talk About It

Have you ever been in a situation like Joseph? Have you ever been treated badly or unfairly? What did you do?

Have an encouraging time of conversation with your family about how to deal with situations that revolve around jealousy, bragging, and unfair treatment. What can you do if you are ever in a circumstance where you are the favorite? How should you respond? What about when you are treated unfairly; how should you respond then?

Take some time to consider these situations in your life and ask God to both help you repent of wrong behavior, and trust Him when you are wronged. You can be an example of God's grace and His faithfulness, if you respond in a proper way.

Dear God, thank You for Your grace and mercy when difficult situations arise. Help me to be a person of peace and be faithful to You, even when I am in a pit. Amen.

Serve One Another

Take the opportunity to think through the situations your family discussed yesterday. What are some tangible ways you can stop jealousy, bragging, and hurting one another? Can you encourage someone instead of reacting out of jealousy? Or can you pray for someone who has hurt you?

By taking the time to identify these actions, you will see how often they occur in the lives around you and what you can do to walk in an opposite action. When you choose good behavior, you give God the opportunity to work out favor in your life. If you struggle on a particular day, write the word "opposite" on your hand to remind yourself how to respond.

Dear God, help me to serve others instead of retaliating. Help me to be a light and a person of change instead of one who continues doing wrong. Amen.

Eat Together

This week's recipe might not be the best for eating, but it can still be good for some fun! Homemade playdough is a staple among young families. Make some from scratch to help you remember God's story of faithfulness to Joseph and his brothers.

You'll need:

1 cup flour
2 tsp cream of tartar
½ cup salt
1 tbsp cooking oil
1 cup water
Food coloring (many colors, like Joseph's robe)

Mix water and food coloring in a large pot. Add the vegetable oil and stir. Add in the flour, cream of tartar, and salt and mix it together thoroughly. Cook on low/medium heat until mixture becomes foamy; soon afterward, it will become dry. When a dough ball begins to take shape, remove the pan from heat. After mixture cools, knead it for five minutes, then play and enjoy!

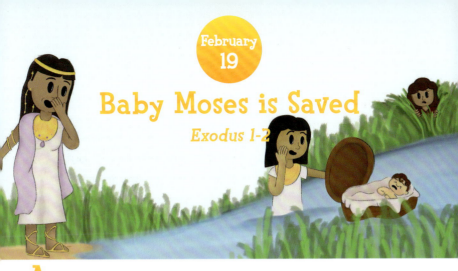

Baby Moses is Saved

Exodus 1-2

February 19

After the time of Joseph had passed, there was a new pharaoh. He was concerned that there were too many Israelites (descendants of Joseph and his father), so he decided to order all baby boys to be killed. One of the baby boys was hidden by his family to save his life. When they could no longer hide him, they put him in a basket and floated him down the Nile River; then Miriam, his sister, waited and watched. The pharaoh's daughter found him and brought him inside the palace. She knew he was an Israelite baby. Miriam emerged from her hiding spot and asked: "Would you like me to find someone to care for this baby?" The pharaoh's daughter said she would like that, so Miriam went to find her mother.

The baby was named Moses, and his mother brought him home and cared for him until he was old enough to return to the palace. Even though Moses was an Israelite boy, God protected him. He grew up safely in the palace.

Dear God, thank You for loving and protecting us, even when we are young. Thank You for your care when we are in danger. Amen.

A Simple Prayer

This month we are celebrating God's love for His children! We have learned that God protected and cared for baby Moses, even in very dangerous circumstances. God knew exactly what needed to happen for Moses to become all God meant for him to be. By recognizing God's favor in difficult times, we can become all He has made us to be and fulfill His plan for our lives, just as Moses did, who was destined to grow up in the palace.

During February, pray this simple prayer with your family, thanking God for His love for you!

Jesus, You are love. Thank You for loving us unconditionally, when we do well and when we fail. Your love for us saves us. Teach us how to cultivate love in our lives and in our relationships with one another. Help us to grow and serve you always. Amen.

February 21

Bible Verse of the Week

"God saw the troubles of the people of Israel, and he was concerned about them" (Exodus 2:25; ICB).

One of the best ways to grow personally and as a family is to memorize Scripture.

This week, we learned how baby Moses' life was saved. We witnessed God's concern and divine protection over him as his life was spared.

Take the time to memorize Exodus 2:25 with your family! Write it out and post it to your refrigerator. Let each person in your family have the opportunity to say it aloud, and then say it all together. Have fun enjoying the Word of God as a family!

Dear God, thank You for the Bible. Help us to memorize Your Word and to hide it in our hearts. Amen.

February 22

Do it!

Moses was too young to realize he was in danger as he floated down the Nile; but if you are reading this with your family, you are old enough to recognize that a baby floating in deep water is a sign of danger. Moses was in danger even before the moment he was placed in the water. He was not old enough to swim on his own. Also, a large animal could have thought baby Moses was food.

Because Moses was young, he likely didn't sense the risk he was wading through. But what if he did realize it? What if you were placed on a boat in the middle of a river? Danger and perceived danger can cause fear and anxiety. Though Moses might not have known what was happening as a baby, we can see God protecting Moses from the beginning. If you are in danger, what do you do? Do you ask God for help?

Just as you might have a plan for when there is a tornado or a storm, you may also need a plan when anxiety, danger, or a threat arrives. Think through situations when you have been anxious or have been in dangerous situation and write out a plan you can follow should this happen again. You may decide to just take a deep breath, or say a prayer, or get help from an adult. Share your plan for danger as a family and remember to take care!

Dear God, thank You for helping me when I am fearful or in danger. Help me to be prepared and to be mindful of Your constant care for me. Amen.

February 23

Talk About It

A good way to give thanks to God is to remember the times He has been faithful on your behalf! As you spend time this week reading through the story of baby Moses, try to think of times that God has kept you safe. What happened? How did God protect you?

We go through life grumbling about things we don't understand. We may complain about a traffic jam, not realizing the delay protected us from an accident up ahead. We may complain about not getting something we want, and then realize God gives us exactly what we need. It's important to examine our lives and be intentionally grateful for the times God has gone ahead of us, protecting us from danger or harm. The next time you are fearful or want to complain, remember the times God has covered you and cared for you.

Dear God, thank You for keeping us safe and protected. Help us to be grateful and remember how good You are. Amen.

February 24

Serve One Another

In the story of Moses this week, we see how Miriam served her brother by sending him down the Nile and then watching him closely. Soon after, the pharaoh's daughter picked Moses up, saved him, and sent Miriam to bring the baby's mother to take him home and care for him. We can also do good things to help others when they are in danger or in need.

Go through your clothes this week. How many pieces of clothing or pairs of shoes do you have that you rarely wear? Is there anything in good condition that you can donate to a homeless shelter or to an organization that helps those in need? Is there anything specific you could buy and donate? There are many people who could use a helping hand or warm clothes this time of year. Intentionally give to others who could use the comfort or safety that your service can bring.

Dear God, help me to be thankful for what I have, and help me to be generous to those who might need a helping hand. Amen.

February 25

Eat Together

Just like Moses was wrapped in a basket and sent down the Nile, we can swaddle a hot dog to enjoy for lunch!

> You will need:
> Hot dogs or Bratwurst
> Buns
> Condiments of choice like ketchup, mustard, beans, etc.
> Potato Chips or side

Boil up some hot dogs or heat them up on the grill. Let everyone in the family nestle one into a bun and top it with their favorite condiments. Surround your hot dog with chips, just like Moses was surrounded by river grass.

Enjoy your family meal and remember all you learned this week about how God cared for baby Moses.

Dear God, thank You for food to eat and for nourishment when we need it. Thank You for providing for our every need, big and small. Amen.

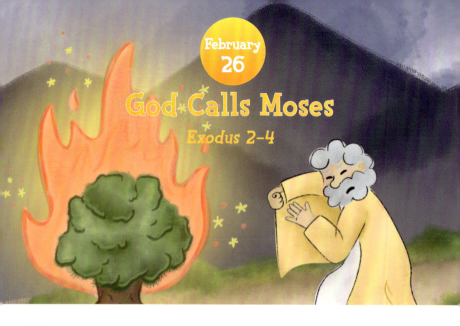

God Calls Moses
Exodus 2–4

February 26

When Moses was an adult, he married a woman named Zipporah. He was helping her father tend to the sheep when God showed up in a burning bush! Can you imagine? As Moses got closer to the bush, he saw that it was on fire but not burning up. God called to Moses from the bush, and he said: "Take off your sandals, because you are standing on holy ground" (Exodus 3:5; NCV). God went on to tell Moses to save the Israelites by leading them out of slavery in Egypt.

Moses doubted himself and made all kinds of excuses as to why he couldn't do it; one of them was that he had a difficult time speaking. But God nudged back and said: "I will be with you." He also sent Moses' brother, Aaron, to go with him. Together, they led the people out of slavery, so they could be free to worship God.

Dear God, thank You for calling Moses and leading the Israelites out of Egypt. Help us listen to Your call when You ask us to serve. Amen.

A Simple Prayer

This month we are celebrating God's love for His children! As we learn about the calling of Moses, we learn that God loves us and believes in us, even when we have doubts. Through faith, we can become all He has made us to be. We can answer His call and find fulfillment in obedience, just as Moses did when he led the Israelites out of Egypt.

During February, pray this simple prayer with your family, thanking God for His love for you!

Jesus, You are love. Thank You for loving us unconditionally, when we do well and when we fail. Your love for us saves us. Teach us how to cultivate love in our lives and in our relationships with one another. Help us to grow and serve you always. Amen.

February 28

Bible Verse of the Week

> "Who gave human beings their mouths?... Is it not, I the lord? Now go, I will help you speak and will teach you what to say" (Exodus 4:11-12; NIV).

One of the best ways to grow personally and as a family is to memorize Scripture.

This week, we learned how God called Moses. We witnessed God's love and faith in him, even when Moses doubted himself.

Take the time to memorize Exodus 4:11–12 with your family! Write it out and post it to your refrigerator. Let each person in your family have the opportunity to say it aloud, and then say it all together. Have fun enjoying the Word of God as a family!

Dear God, thank You for the Bible. Help us to memorize Your Word and to hide it in our hearts. Amen.

March 1

Do it!

Sometimes God calls us to do things that make us a little nervous. Moses was scared when God asked him to lead the people out of Egypt. He felt unequipped and insecure, and he was fearful that he would have a hard time speaking. But God replied to Moses' fear by saying: "Who made a person's mouth? . . . It is I, the Lord . . . I will help . . . you and . . . teach you what to do" (Exodus 4:11, 15; NCV)."

Have you ever felt God call you to something that made you feel uncomfortable? Sometimes when we need our faith to be stretched, God must teach us something new and out of our normal routine. Think of something that you would like to try that you haven't done before. Maybe it's speaking in front of a group, or praying aloud, or drawing something by hand. Give something new a try today and see what happens! You won't be an expert on your first try; but God is with you. So have some fun!

Dear God, thank You for being with us. Thank You for stretching our faith and for asking us to try new things. Amen.

March 2

Talk About It

Today is a day to dream. Sit down with your family and talk about some of the things you enjoy in your life. What are the activities you love doing? Write them down.

Did you know that God can use the things you love doing to show the world His love? Moses led people out of slavery in Egypt by witnessing God's greatness to Egyptians and Israelites alike. We all need to hear the stories of God's greatness and intervention; by doing so, we encourage one another to thrive. Through sharing our testimonies and our joy, we can inspire one another to live for God. Even if you aren't living in unjust conditions like the Israelites were, we all need community and the support of one another. By enjoying your life in Jesus, you can share your gifts and faith with others.

Dear God, thank You for giving us things to enjoy doing on this Earth! Help us to share our talents, hobbies, and gifts with others so we can encourage one another. Amen.

March 3

Serve One Another

Today is a day to serve the members of your family. Moses and Aaron served the Israelites by leading them out of Egypt; you can serve others in your family by helping to lighten the load.

Ask your mom or dad how you can help them today. Do your best to serve them by helping in any way they need. Moms and dads have a lot on their chore lists every single day. Taking care of a home, car, family, and pets can be very tiring! Making the offer to help and serve them will bring a smile to their faces.

Dear God, remind me to offer to help out more often. Give me opportunities to serve my parents and the people in my family. Amen.

Eat Together

As a reminder of the burning bush, you can enjoy some spicy (or mild) salsa today as a family!

You will need:

2 (15oz) cans fire-roasted tomatoes or use 4 cups chopped fresh tomatoes (1 ¾ pounds)

1/3 cup chopped white or sweet onion

2 medium cloves garlic

1 to 2 medium jalapeño or serrano peppers (optional)

1 to 2 medium limes (juiced)

1 cup chopped fresh cilantro

1/2 teaspoon fine sea salt to taste

1 bag of tortilla chips

Chop up cilantro, onions, garlic, and peppers in a food processor.

Add tomatoes, lime juice, and salt.

Pulse until it is the consistency you like.

Grab a bag of tortilla chips and enjoy!

Dear God, thank You for feeding us with good food and for calling us to serve You. Help us to have faith and believe in You. Amen.

God Splits the Red Sea
Exodus 4–15

March 5

Moses and Aaron went to Egypt to do as God told them and lead the Israelites out of bondage. They appeared before Pharaoh and requested that he release the Israelites. Pharaoh's heart was hardened. He wouldn't let the Israelites go, so God sent plague after plague to change his mind. He sent frogs, gnats, flies, sickness, death and more, but Pharaoh was stubborn. After the last plague of death, Pharaoh finally let the people go.

Moses and Aaron led the Israelites to the Red Sea and set up camp for the night. Pharaoh changed his mind about letting the slaves go and sent his army to go get them back. The Israelites heard them coming and thought they were going to die, but Moses prayed and stretched out his staff over the sea. The sea split in half, and the Israelites were able to walk across the dry sea bed! Pharoah sent his army after them, but just as the Israelites reached the other side, Moses stretched out his staff one more time, and the sea came back together to drown their enemies. The Israelites praised God for protecting them.

Dear God, thank You for making a way where there is no way. Thank You for your faithfulness and protection. Amen.

March 6

A Simple Prayer

This month, we are increasing our faith in God! As we consider the splitting of the Red Sea, we learn that God fights for us and protects us, even when we have doubts. By receiving God's salvation when He provides for us, we are free to praise and worship Him fully, just like Moses and the Israelites.

During March, pray this simple prayer with your family, thanking God for the faith He has made available for you!

Jesus, we want to believe in You with our whole hearts. Thank You for being faithful to us! Teach us how to cultivate faith in our lives and in our relationships with You. Help us to grow and serve you always. Amen.

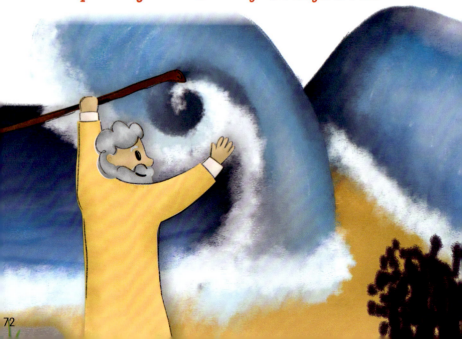

March 7

Bible Verse of the Week

> "The lord himself will fight for you. Just stay calm" (Exodus 14:14; NLT).

One of the best ways to grow personally and as a family is to memorize Scripture.

This week, we learned how God split the Red Sea. We discovered God's love and protection over Moses and the Israelites through His miraculous provision!

Take the time to memorize Exodus 14:14 with your family! Write it out and post it to your refrigerator. Let each person in your family have the opportunity to say it aloud, and then say it all together. Have fun enjoying the Word of God as a family!

Dear God, thank You for the Bible. Help us to memorize Your Word and to hide it in our hearts. Amen.

March 8
Do it!

We've all faced some scary or difficult things; we may have encountered situations that seemed impossible. It is unlikely that Moses and the Israelites would ever have imagined that God would part the Red Sea, but He did! When Moses cried out to God, God did the miraculous.

If you are going through a hard time, find a few Bible verses that can encourage you. Write them down and keep them in a place where you can look at them often. If you aren't going through anything too difficult at this time, go to your Bible anyway and find some Bible verses that will help you when you do! Write them down, put them in an envelope, and label the envelope "Be encouraged." Set the envelope somewhere you can easily find it when you need it.

Dear God, thank You for being there for us when we need You. Remind us to go to the Bible for answers and encouragement. Amen.

Talk About It

This week we have been learning about how God rescued the Israelites from Pharaoh's army. Besides this week's passage, what are some Bible stories you love about God fighting for His people? How have they encouraged you? Think about times God has protected and fought for you in your real life. What happened then?

Sit together with your family and share these stories. Enjoy talking about God's good and perfect provision for us. God loves His children and goes to extreme lengths to show it! It's wonderful when we share those testimonies and celebrate together.

Dear God, thank You for your mercy, grace, and protection. Thank You for always showing up for us. Amen.

March 10

Serve One Another

You might not need a Red Sea parted in your house, but there are other situations involving water that you could pray about and act upon! How about starting a load of dishes in the dishwasher? You could help a younger sibling take a bath. Do you have any indoor plants that you could water?

These may seem too simple, but small things really are big things once we add them all up. God used Moses to bring about a huge miracle that brought help to a multitude of people. We may not be able to do something this big; but we can do little things around the house that can help those around us. These small things refresh our surroundings and keep us from being idle. Try it and see how good it feels after you complete one of these small chores. Then thank God for the opportunity for a small win during your day.

Dear God, thank You for small wins and big wins. You are the best miracle we could ask for. Help us to be diligent in serving You and each other. Amen.

March 11

Eat Together

Who doesn't love a little Jello™?

> You'll need:
>
> A red or blue packet of Jello™
>
> Pretzels, chips, or finger food

Grab a packet of your favorite flavor of Jello™ and prepare it with your family according to the directions. After it has chilled, everyone should grab a spoon and sit together on one side of the bowl. Place your pretzels, chips, or finger food on the opposite side of the bowl. Everyone then takes turns scooping up spoons of Jello from the center until they have created a path from one side to the other. It's like you are parting the Red Sea. Once finished, everyone can enjoy the snack on the other side.

Celebrate God's faithfulness together!

Dear God, thank You for Your faithfulness to us. You are good, and we are grateful. Amen.

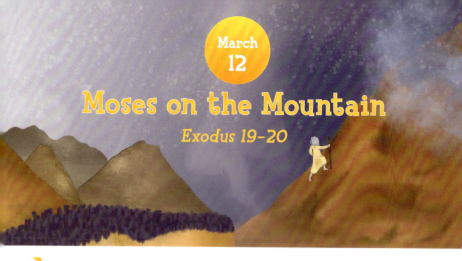

March 12

Moses on the Mountain
Exodus 19–20

After the Red Sea parted, Moses and the Israelites walked to the other side. They continued walking for a long while until they got to the tallest mountain in all of Egypt. Once there, Moses climbed all the way to the top of the mountain so he could talk with God. God reminded Moses of His faithfulness and told Moses He had several commandments the Israelites needed to follow. If they could obey the commandments, they would always respect God and one another, and they would be a healthy family.

Moses relayed the message to the Israelites, and they wanted to know what commandments they had to follow. So, Moses went back up the mountain to hear from God again. Thunder and lightning occurred, and Moses came back down the mountain with two stone tablets on which God had written the ten laws (or commandments) that He wanted the people to follow. Open your Bible to Exodus 20 and read through them as a family.

Dear God, thank You for the Ten Commandments and for showing us how to honor You and honor others. Help us to obey them to the best of our ability. Amen.

March 13

A Simple Prayer

This month, we are increasing our faith in God!

As we learn about the Ten Commandments, we learn that God gives us everything we need to live a life of faith in Him. By receiving God's wisdom in the Ten Commandments, we can honor God and others fully, just as Moses and the Israelites.

During March, pray this simple prayer with your family, thanking God for the faith He has made available for you!

Jesus, we want to believe in You with our whole hearts. Thank You for being faithful to us! Teach us how to cultivate faith in our lives and in our relationships with one another. Help us to grow and serve you always. Amen.

March 14

Bible Verse of the Week

One of the best ways to grow personally and as a family is to memorize Scripture.

This week, we learned how God gave Moses the Ten Commandments. We saw God's care through the story of the Israelites and His instructions made it clear how to honor Him and honor others!

Take the time to memorize Exodus 19:5 with your family! Write it out and post it to your refrigerator. Let each person in your family have the opportunity to say it aloud, and then say it all together. Have fun enjoying the Word of God as a family!

Dear God, thank You for the Bible. Help us to memorize Your Word and to hide it in our hearts. Amen.

"Now if you obey me fully and keep my covenant, then out of all nations you will be my treasured possession" (Exodus 19:5; NIV).

Do it!

Have you heard of the Ten Commandments before today? You may have heard of them at Sunday School or church; or perhaps this is the first time you have heard about them. Either way, do you think you and your family can memorize all ten of them?

Take an index card or piece of paper and see how many you can remember! Here's a hint: there are four commandments about loving God and six about loving others. You can check your answers below:

1. You must have no other god but Me.
2. Do not make idols to worship.
3. Do not misuse My name.
4. Dedicate one day a week to resting and worshiping Me.
5. Honor your father and mother.
6. Do not kill each other.
7. Be faithful to your wife and husband.
8. Do not steal from each other.
9. Do not lie to each other.
10. Do not be jealous of each other.

Dear God, thank You for helping us memorize the Ten Commandments. Help us to honor them in our daily lives. Amen.

March 16

Talk About It

Sit around the table with your family today and spend some time talking about the Ten Commandments. Which of them are easy to keep? Why? Which of them are more difficult to keep? Why?

Do you think it's possible to keep all ten of the commandments all the time?

It's pretty nice that God narrowed everything down to the top ten things we need to do to honor Him and to honor others. If you ever start to feel overwhelmed by life, just remember that God has listed the most important things here for you! You can be sure that doing your best to obey these ten commands will result in living a life that God will bless. He was gracious enough to simplify His rules for us, so we can be thoughtful enough to do our best to follow through!

Dear God, thank You for loving us through the Ten Commandments and for simplifying what You desire for us. Amen.

March 17

Serve One Another

Witnessing others doing good can encourage us to do good as well. Take every opportunity this week to do good; make it a priority to watch for other family members doing good. If you happen to notice that your brother or sister followed one of the Ten Commandments, write down what happened. If you do something that you know honored the Ten Commandments, write that down, too!

Keep a pile of well-followed commandments on the kitchen counter this week and see how many you can pile up! By honoring the Ten Commandments, you are serving God and serving each other. You can celebrate all the good done this week by reading through each day's cards together as a family!

Dear God, help us to remember to do good this week and to serve You and our families while doing so. Help us to bless one another. Amen.

Eat Together

Time to make some stone tablets together (and then eat them)!

You'll need:
6 cups of Rice Krispies™
3 Tbs Butter
10 oz bag of marshmallows

In a large saucepan, melt butter over low heat. Add marshmallows and stir until completely melted. Remove the saucepan from heat and set aside.

Add Rice Krispies™ cereal until well-coated with marshmallow mixture. Press into a 9x9 pan or flatten onto waxed paper. Allow to set, then cut the Rice Krispies™ Treats into shapes as you imagine the Ten Commandments stone tablets may have looked. While enjoying this small treat, talk about this week's lesson together as a family.

Dear God, You are wise and faithful! Thank You for teaching us this week. Help us to love You and others in all that we do. Amen.

Exploring Canaan
Numbers 13–14

The Israelites traveled far and long; then they finally arrived near the land of Canaan, the place the Bible calls the Promised Land—a land flowing with milk and honey. Israel was made up of twelve groups or tribes. God instructed Moses to send one man from each of the twelve tribes to scout out the land. They found luscious fruit like grapes, pomegranates, and figs. They took some back to the Israelites and told them about all they saw.

The land was good, and the fruit was amazing, but the people in the land were huge! Almost all the men were too frightened to enter. The Israelites complained, "Why did God bring us all the way here just to be defeated? We want to go back to Egypt!" But two of the men, Joshua and Caleb, believed that if God was pleased with them, then He would give them the land.

Moses and Aaron went to their place of worship and prayed. The people's anger grew and they were ready to begin throwing stones. Suddenly, the glory of God filled the place of worship. Moses begged God to forgive the people. God forgave them, but only Joshua and Caleb were allowed to enter the Promised Land. The rest of the Israelites had to wander around the wilderness for forty years and never see the land flowing with milk and honey.

Dear God, thank You for fulfilling Your promises to us. Help us to keep the faith and continue to be brave. Amen.

March 20
A Simple Prayer

This month we are increasing our faith in God! As we learn about the promises in Canaan, we learn that God gives us everything we need to live a life of faith in Him. By finally making it to our Promised Land (the place God has prepared for us to possess in life), we can enter with courage and thanksgiving! When we honor God and live out the faith He gives us, we can be just like Joshua and Caleb.

During March, pray this simple prayer with your family, thanking God for the faith He has made available for you!

Jesus, we want to believe in You with our whole hearts. Thank You for being faithful to us! Teach us how to cultivate faith in our lives and in our relationships with one another. Help us to grow and serve you always. Amen.

March 21

Bible Verse of the Week

"If the lord is pleased with us, he will lead us into that land, a land flowing with milk and honey, and will give it to us" (Numbers 14:8; NIV).

One of the best ways to grow personally and as a family is to memorize Scripture.

This week, we learned how God brought the Israelites to Canaan—the Promised Land. We encountered God's faithfulness as His presence filled the place of worship.

Take the time to memorize Numbers 14:8 with your family! Write it out and post it to your refrigerator. Let each person in your family have the opportunity to say it aloud, and then say it all together. Have fun enjoying the Word of God as a family!

Dear God, thank You for the Bible. Help us to memorize Your Word and to hide it in our hearts. Amen.

March 22

Do it!

Have you ever complained to God? Sometimes, when God gives us results that are different from what we've prayed for or different than we expected, we can get frustrated. The Israelites definitely got angry when they thought they were going to be defeated by giants and never get to enter the Promised Land. When they complained and were ready to start throwing stones, God's glory filled the place of worship.

The Israelites ended up losing their opportunity to enter the land, except for Joshua and Caleb. The others had to wander around in the wilderness for 40 years!

Can you think of a time when you wanted to complain and be frustrated with God? Gratitude can calm us down and remind us of God's faithfulness. Spend today making a gratitude list of all the ways God has come through for you. They can be big things or little things; regardless, He deserves thanks and praise!

Dear God, thank You for Your constant faithfulness and provision. Help us to remember how You have always chosen us and how You always come through for us. Amen.

March 23
Talk About It

As we've been following the Israelites journey through the wilderness and to the Promised Land of Canaan, you've likely noticed how the people complained, were scared, made mistakes, and even wanted to go back to Egypt. Many times in our lives, we react in the same way. Sometimes it's easy to think God has forgotten us, or He's given us something too difficult to handle. We can get frustrated and start to lose faith.

But God always provides; and we need to celebrate when He does!

Can you think of a time God provided for you or your family when you really needed it? What did you need? And what did God do? Did He provide a friend or finances? Did He bring you comfort or help? Talk about the ways God has been good to your family. It helps us to remember when God proved His love to us by caring for us when we really needed it.

Dear God, thank You for caring for us. Increase our faith in You as we celebrate the goodness of Your provisions! Amen.

Serve One Another

We learned this week that God allowed Joshua and Caleb to go to the Promised Land, but he also made the rest of the Israelites wander in the wilderness for forty years. God knew it wasn't the best for them, but He always leaves His people with the option of whether or not to choose Him. It seems it all came down to faith . . . or the lack of it!

What are some of the ways you can show others encouragement this week? Can you make a phone call to a grandparent? Maybe you can write your parents a nice note. Can you draw a picture for a friend with a Bible verse attached? Is there someone you can pray for who is struggling?

A small act of encouragement on your part might be just the thing to bring faith to a family member or friend. Do something today that will help someone get to their Promised Land—the special place God has for them.

Dear God, thank You for hope and your encouragement to us in difficult times. Help us to move forward with faith and peace. Amen.

March 25

Eat Together

This week's recipe is rather simple, but it is luscious and delicious! The Israelites saw grapes, pomegranates, and figs in Canaan; you can find these fruits at the grocery store! Grab some of the freshest grapes, perhaps a box of fig cookies, and some pomegranate juice. Take your time to smell and then taste each one, experiencing what it might have been like to enter Canaan.

Which one is your favorite? Why? Every time you have one of these items from now on, remember the faith God has set aside for you. Rejoice in His provision for you!

Dear God, thank You for the fruit that lasts—the good things that come from you. Help us to have a deepened faith to know You better. Amen.

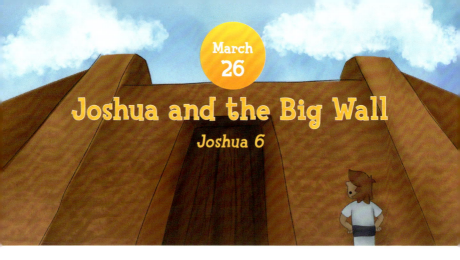

March 26

Joshua and the Big Wall
Joshua 6

The Israelites had wandered in the wilderness forty years until an entire generation had passed away, including Moses. Joshua became the leader of the younger generation. As they entered the Promised Land of Canaan, they arrived at a city named Jericho. It had a huge wall surrounding it that was guarded by soldiers. Even though the city seemed impossible to conquer, God instructed Joshua to lead the Israelites in a march around the city once a day for six days. The priests were to carry seven ram's horns and march in front of the Ark of the Covenant, the golden box that held the Ten Commandments. On the seventh day, they were to march around the city seven times. On the seventh time around, they were to blow their horns and then shout. God told Joshua that when they did, the wall would fall.

Even though the instructions seemed strange, Joshua and the Israelites did as God instructed them. Sure enough, the wall fell down! The Israelites finally got to enter Jericho under Joshua's leadership. Yet again, God had kept His promise.

Dear God, thank You for wise instructions. Help us to follow Your guidance and trust in You. Amen.

March 27

A Simple Prayer

This month, we are increasing our faith in God! As we learn about Joshua's leadership and obedience to God in Jericho, we can grow in our faith, too. When arriving in Jericho, the Israelites might have felt discouraged by the large wall. But God gave clear instructions, and the Israelites obeyed by faith. When they did, that wall came down!

During March, pray this simple prayer with your family, thanking God for the faith He has made available for you!

Jesus, we want to believe in You with our whole hearts. Thank You for being faithful to us! Teach us how to cultivate faith in our lives and in our relationships with one another. Help us to grow and serve you always. Amen.

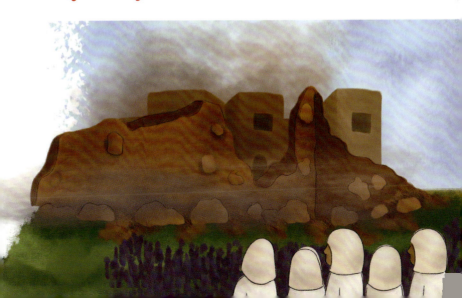

March 28

Bible Verse of the Week

One of the best ways to grow personally and as a family is to memorize Scripture.

We have learned how God instructed Joshua and the Israelites to bring the wall down in Jericho. We saw God's faithfulness as His instructions proved successful.

Take the time to memorize Isaiah 55:8–9 with your family! Write it out and post it to your refrigerator. Let each person in your family have the opportunity to say it aloud, and then say it all together. Have fun enjoying the Word of God as a family!

Dear God, thank You for the Bible. Help us to memorize Your Word and to hide it in our hearts. Amen.

"For my thoughts are not your thoughts, neither are your ways my ways,' declares the LORD. As the heavens are higher than the earth, so are my ways higher than your ways and my thoughts than your thoughts'" (Isaiah 55:8-9; NIV).

March 29

Do It!

Maybe there isn't an actual giant wall around your house, or your neighborhood, or your church, but that doesn't mean you can't follow God's instructions to pray and shout to bring down anything that is holding you and your community captive. Praying and walking at the same time can be one of the best ways to hear God's voice and to talk with Him. As you do, you can bless your family, pray for your neighbors, and encourage your church.

Take a prayer walk today as a family. Even if it's just for five minutes, use those five minutes for the glory of God. Declare His goodness in your community, and practice being obedient to what the Ten Commandments have taught you!

Dear God, please be with us as we pray and walk. Let Your presence lead us as we bless our community. Amen.

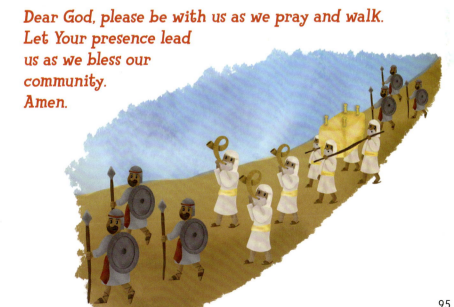

March 30
Talk About It

You may remember another story you studied as a family in January in which God gave His people instructions. Can you guess who? If you said, Noah, then congratulations! Just like Joshua was given clear instructions by God that may have seemed strange at the time, we also remember God instructing Noah to build a large boat. It seems like God may know that we need our faith tested from time to time. Why do you think God tests our faith?

Have you ever gotten instructions from God that you felt were a little strange? What did you do? Did you follow through with them or not? Talk about it with your family and enjoy the time of fellowship over the big and little steps of faith in your lives.

Dear God, You are so faithful to us! Help us to always be grateful, listen closely, and thank You often. Amen.

Serve One Another

Is there an empty wall in your house that isn't getting much love? If so, see if you can find a stack of sticky notes. Whenever you feel discouraged or hear of someone with a need, write a Bible verse or a prayer on the sticky note and stick it to the wall. Every time you pass by the wall, pray for one of the needs and then thank God for His faithfulness! After several weeks, go back to the wall and review your prayer requests, prayers, and Bible verses.

How did God show up? How does your heart feel after exercising your faith in a practical way?

Dear God, help us to remember to talk with You. We want to give You our hearts, prayer, needs, and friends. Amen.

Eat Together

This week's snack involves a bit of a challenge! Using only what you can find in your pantry or refrigerator, find food items with which you can build a wall. It can be crackers and peanut butter, waffles and syrup, or anything worth using.

When you get all the supplies you need, sit down at the table to create a Jericho scene. You can be fancy or silly; you can add trumpets or the Ten Commandments. Let your imagination lead you. While you build your project, talk with your family about all you learned this week. Share about God's faithfulness to provide as you enjoy your snack!

Dear God, thank You for teaching us about how good You are this week. You are loving, faithful, and strong. Amen.

Gideon and the Tiny Army
Judges 6–7

Over two hundred years after Joshua led Israel into the Promised Land—the land of Canaan, there was a boy named Gideon whose life was made difficult by a group of Midianites who lived just east of Canaan. The Midianites ravaged crops and stole herds so that Gideon and the Israelites were very hungry. One day, an angel of the Lord came to Gideon and said, "The lord is with you, mighty warrior." Gideon was shocked because he believed he was the weakest in his family. But the angel told him that God had a very special job for him to do.

God told Gideon he would defeat the Midianites as long as he followed God's instructions. After Gideon gathered the army, God had him decrease its size by watching the soldiers drink water from a spring. If they cupped the water with their hands, they were able to keep their eyes on their surroundings. This showed they were good soldiers. God told Gideon to send everyone else home. This made Gideon's army small but mighty. Only 300 men entered the Midianite camp, but this small force prevailed and sent the Midianites scampering.

This proved to the Israelites, once again, that God was trustworthy.

Dear God, thank You that we can always depend on You. Help us to know that You are our strength, no matter the size of our support system. Amen.

April 3

A Simple Prayer

This month, we are learning to trust God and receive His peace. When we take the time to reflect on the fact that we can fully rely on God and trust His instructions, we can begin to know His peace. By obeying God, we can experience all He has for us and share His abundant provision with others.

During April, pray this simple prayer with your family, thanking God for His peace in you!

Jesus, You are the Prince of Peace. Thank You for giving us courage in place of fear, confidence in place of insecurity, and peace in place of worry. Teach us to cultivate peace in our lives and in our relationships with one another. Help us to grow and serve you always. Amen.

April 4

Bible Verse of the Week

*"I lift my eyes to the mountains—where does my help come from? My help comes from the L*ORD*, the Maker of heaven and earth" (Psalm 121:1-2; NIV).*

One of the best ways to grow personally and as a family is to memorize Scripture.

We have learned how Gideon defeated the Midianites. We witnessed God's instruction to Gideon and his success!

Take the time to memorize Psalm 121:1–2 with your family! Write it out and post it to your refrigerator. Let each person in your family have the opportunity to say it aloud, and then say it all together. Have fun enjoying the Word of God as a family!

Dear God, thank You for the Bible. Help us to memorize Your Word and to hide it in our hearts. Amen.

April 5

Do it!

How would you feel if God called you to fight like He called Gideon? Gideon was nervous because he believed he was the weakest in his family and not likely to win. But the Angel of the Lord persisted, and Gideon followed through with God's request. And then he won!

Pretend you are Gideon today. Draw a picture of yourself in full armor. Give yourself plenty of time to make up the details of your outfit. Share your picture with your family and give everyone a chance to explain their drawing.

Relish in the fact that God qualifies those He calls. You can celebrate that God comes through, and you can trust Him!

Dear God, thank You for giving us courage when we don't feel courageous. Help us to follow through with Your instructions. Amen.

Talk About It

Spend some time today talking about what it might be like to be Gideon. Do you think you would have the courage to follow through with God as Gideon did? Maybe you are the youngest in your family or you may feel like the weakest member; what if God told you that He had a special assignment for you? How do you think you would respond?

Encourage one another in prayer today as you think through some circumstances in your lives that might feel like the ravaging of the Midianites. Pray for each other that each one of you would have boldness, strength, wisdom, and the courage only God can give.

Dear God, You are strong and faithful. Remind us to pray and to be encouraged by You. Amen.

April 7

Serve One Another

Think of an area in your house that gets neglected or stays consistently messy. Just like the Midianites devoured the resources of the Israelites, your procrastination may be causing an area of your home from being the resource it could be Take twenty minutes to go through that pile of mail, or reorganize the shoe closet, sweep out the laundry room, or whatever you need to do! Serve your entire family by completing a task you dread; in so doing, you can make a disorganized part of your home into a blessing instead of it being devoured by dysfunction.

Once you have completed the task, share your feelings with your family. Do you feel refreshed and revitalized? Do you feel accomplished? How are you going to use your new space and make sure that it doesn't go back to being messy? Just like you got rid of some clutter to minimize your mess, God had Gideon minimize his army in order to bring success. Small changes make a big difference!

Dear God, thank You for helping us when we want to procrastinate. Thank You for motivating us to clear out the clutter in our hearts and lives. Amen.

Eat Together

Gideon and his family must have been really discouraged when their crops and cattle were being devoured by the Midianites. Spend today building a salad with your favorite vegetables. Thank God as you add each ingredient.

As you pile onto your plate all the vegetables that will help you strengthen your body, thank God for all the ways He has provided and protected you. Spend time celebrating all the good things in your life as you share your salad with your family.

Dear God, thank You for all that You provide. When difficulties come our way, help us to be like Gideon and respond to Your instructions. Amen.

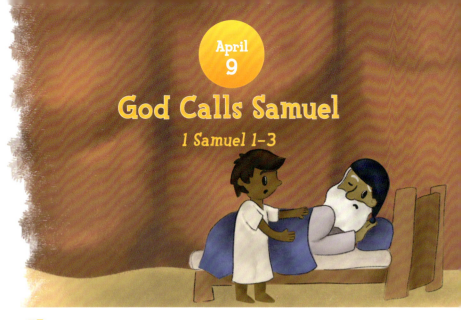

April 9

God Calls Samuel
1 Samuel 1–3

Hundreds of years after Gideon fought the Midianites, a man named Elkanah and a woman named Hannah worshiped God in the temple. Hannah was unable to have children, and she cried out to the Lord, "You know that I can't have children. If You gave me a son, I would give him back to You."

Hannah became pregnant, and she and Elkanah followed through with their promise to the Lord. When their baby, Samuel, was no longer an infant, she took him to the temple where she had prayed to God. Eli the priest took Samuel in and taught him how to serve God. Hannah and Elkanah came to see Samuel each year. God blessed their faithfulness by giving them more children.

One evening while asleep, Samuel heard someone calling his name. He thought it was the priest, Eli; but Eli told Samuel to respond to the voice with, "I'm listening, Lord." Samuel did so, and God shared with him the plans for Israel. Eventually, Samuel would replace Eli as priest, and he would serve the Lord and the people.

April 10

A Simple Prayer

This month we are learning to trust God and receive His peace. Hannah could not have children, so she cried out to God for a son. She offered to give him back to God, should He allow her to conceive.

Hannah's example teaches us how to fully rely on God and follow through with our actions. By worshiping God, we receive the peace that only He can give us. When we receive peace from Him, we can share His provision with others and serve God faithfully, as Samuel did.

During April, pray this simple prayer with your family, thanking God for His peace in you!

Jesus, You are the Prince of peace. Thank You for giving us courage instead of fear, confidence instead of insecurity, and peace instead of worry. Teach us to steward peace in our lives and in our relationships with one another. Help us to grow and serve you always. Amen.

April 11

Bible Verse of the Week

One of the best ways to grow personally and as a family is to memorize Scripture.

In today's devotional, we learned how God gave Hannah a son, Samuel. We witnessed God's care and Hannah's worship.

Take the time to memorize 1 Samuel 3:10 with your family! Write it out and post it to your refrigerator. Have each person in your family say it aloud, and then say it all together. Have fun enjoying the Word of God as a family!

Dear God, thank You for the Bible. Help us to memorize Your Word and to hide it in our hearts. Amen.

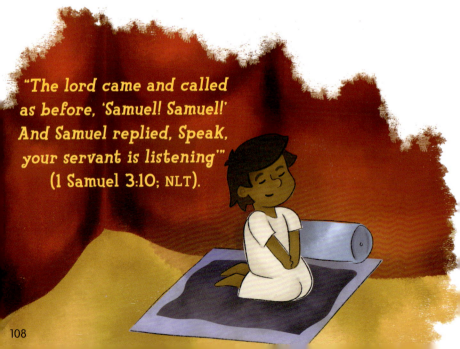

"The lord came and called as before, 'Samuel! Samuel!' And Samuel replied, Speak, your servant is listening'" (1 Samuel 3:10; NLT).

April 12

Do it!

Just as God had a plan for Samuel to serve Him and the people of Israel, God also has a plan for you! Doing good works is how we can actively show others how God lives and moves in us. What are you called to do? In what ways do you serve the Lord in your daily life? What ways would you like to serve God in the future?

Take the time today to purposefully serve God in your home or neighborhood. Perhaps plant flowers or vegetables for someone, walk someone's dog, mow a lawn for a neighbor, or pick up trash in your community. By doing the work God has asked of us, no matter how big or how small, we receive peace in our souls. Matthew 5:14–16 says that good deeds have an evangelistic effect. By doing good work and letting your light shine, you serve God and others.

Look for something to do for God and others today and pay attention to what God does through you!

Dear God, thank You for giving us peace as we do good work. Thank You for giving us the opportunity to serve You and others. Amen.

Talk About It

In this week's lesson, God spoke to Samuel. Have you ever heard God's voice? What did it sound like? How did you know it was Him?

Sit with your family this week and enjoy sharing stories with one another about how God has spoken to you. What did you do after He spoke to you? How did you respond? Just like Samuel said to God, "I'm listening, Lord," you can also stop and purposefully listen. After you share together, pause and pray with one another making room for silence, allowing God to speak into your hearts. Ask God to confirm His directions with the Bible.

Dear God, thank You for speaking to us. Help us to hear You clearly and love You and others in return. Amen.

Serve One Another

Having children is a blessing from God. Sometimes women who want children are not able to have them, and it can cause heartache. Other times, women may have a baby but not have the resources to take care of him or her. Find a local pregnancy center where you can donate diapers or drop off baby clothes for women and children in need. By serving women and helping them care for themselves and their babies, you are serving God. Say a blessing over them and ask God to bring them comfort and good work.

Dear God, please bless mothers. Help young mothers and mothers in need care for themselves and their children well. Amen.

Eat Together

Eating together is a wonderful way to remember God's goodness.

This week, we learned about Hannah and Samuel. We read that Samuel was lying in bed when God first spoke to him. To celebrate this story, grab a stalk of celery, peanut butter or almond butter (or a butter of your choice), and raisins.

Wash and cut the celery into two inch pieces. Pretending it's a bed, spread butter into the celery. Lay "Samuel" down as a raisin in the butter, and remember that God speaks to us, even when we may be trying to sleep! Enjoy the simple treat and nourishment and celebrate God's voice in your everyday life.

Dear God, we worship You today. Thank You for nourishing us and speaking to us this week with Samuel's story. Amen.

David Fights a Giant
1 Samuel 17

April 16

In the city of Bethlehem, there was a shepherd boy named David caring for his sheep. An army of Philistines arrived to fight the Israelites there, and they brought a nine-foot-tall giant with them! The giant bragged that no one could beat him, and he challenged anyone to come and fight against him. Many of the Israelites were scared and didn't want to fight him, but David did!

David wasn't fearful and didn't like the giant's insults against the people. King Saul sent for him because he had heard that David wasn't afraid to fight. He eventually allowed David to fight the giant and then offered his royal armor to David for protection. David decided he could fight better without the armor and went to a river to gather five, smooth stones for his sling.

David arrived to fight the giant, Goliath, with his stones and sling. He said "You come at me with a sword and a spear, but I come at you in the name of the God of Israel!" He spun his sling, and the stone hit Goliath right between the eyes! David won against the giant!

Dear God, thank You for the faith and bravery of David. Help us to be like him and to fear not! Amen.

A Simple Prayer

This month we are learning to trust God and receive His peace. David knew God's peace as he was not fearful to fight Goliath. David's story teaches us how to fully rely on Him and to be brave in the God of Israel. By walking in faith, we receive the peace that only He can give us. When we do, we can share that provision with others, just like David did when he defeated Goliath!

During April, pray this simple prayer with your family, thanking God for His peace in you!

Jesus, You are the Prince of peace. Thank You for giving us courage in place of fear, confidence in place of insecurity, and peace in place of worry. Teach us to cultivate peace in our lives and in our relationships with one another. Help us to grow and serve you always. Amen.

April 18

Bible Verse of the Week

One of the best ways to grow personally and as a family is to memorize Scripture.

We have learned this week how David bravely fought Goliath. We witnessed God's provision as David came at the giant with a prayer and a stone! Take the time to memorize Psalm 37:39 with your family! Write it out and post it to your refrigerator. Let each person in your family have the opportunity to say it aloud, and then say it all together. Have fun enjoying the Word of God as a family!

Dear God, thank You for the Bible. Help us to memorize Your Word and to hide it in our hearts. Amen.

"The Lord rescues the godly; he is their fortress in times of trouble" (Psalm 37:39; NLT).

April 19

Do it!

What do you think you would do if you were threatened a big giant? Do you think you'd be scared or brave?

This week, let's bring this story into reality by getting out the measuring tape! Take a moment and measure the height of every person in your family. Who is the tallest? Who is the smallest?

Now, go outside, and find a tree. Take the measuring tape all the way to the nine-foot mark. This is likely how tall Goliath was! How would you react if you had to come up against someone this tall? Use this opportunity to let the Bible come to life by seeing just how much bigger Goliath is than you. Even though Goliath was big, David's faith was bigger!

Dear God, You are even bigger than Goliath! Help us to believe in You and not to be scared when we encounter the enemies in our lives. Amen.

Talk About It

This week, we've been learning about how big God is, even when we are small. Can you think of several problems or fears in your life that make you feel small? Write them down on a piece of paper. Share those fears or problems with your family.

After everyone has had a chance to share, spend a few minutes talking about each of those fears or problems. Pray together that God would give each of you faith and courage like David. Ask God to help you solve the problems in front of you or help you walk with courage through the fearful situations you might encounter. Rip up your pieces of paper as a sign that nothing can defeat you when God is on your side.

Dear God, You are bigger than any of our fears or problems. Help us to listen to your voice and be encouraged by You. Amen.

April 21
Serve Together

In much the same way that David served the people of Israel by killing Goliath, you can also serve the people around you by trusting God and being brave! Oftentimes, the things that are difficult in our lives are actually what help shape our life stories and testimonies about Jesus. By trusting God and watching Him come through for you, you get to be part of the story God wants others to know.

Go outside and collect a few stones. Bring them back inside and clean them up. Put a jar in an open part of your house where you can drop a stone each time you are brave or face something you fear. As the weeks go by, watch it fill up. Find encouragement by asking your family members to share their bravery when you see them drop a stone in the jar. By sharing how we overcome, we serve each of our family members with our testimonies of Jesus.

Dear God, as we walk with You, remind us to share our stories with one another. Help us to encourage and lift up one another. Amen.

April 22

Eat Together

Make some oatmeal powerballs with your family this week. They can remind you of David's smooth stones!

You'll need:
1 cup old fashioned oats
⅔ cup shredded coconut
½ cup peanut butter (or almond butter)
½ cup ground flaxseed
½ cup chocolate chips
⅓ cup honey

Stir all the ingredients together in a large mixing bowl. Cover and chill the mixing bowl in the refrigerator for 1–2 hours. Roll the mixture into 1-inch balls. Serve and eat.

Dear God, thank You for fighting our battles with us! You make us strong and brave. Amen.

Jonathan Helps His Best Friend
1 Samuel 18, 20

After David won his confrontation with Goliath, he became best friends with Jonathan, King Saul's son. King Saul made David a military leader, but soon got very jealous of David because he had been winning battles and becoming a well-known leader in Israel. King Saul, who wasn't following God, came up with a plan to kill David. He was concerned that the people loved David more and would want him to be their king.

When David realized King Saul's plan, he asked Jonathan to help him. David hid to escape King Saul. Jonathan, who was aware that King Saul was trying to kill David, proved to be a faithful friend. He helped David leave Israel in safety. David and Jonathan promised to be loyal friends to one another forever.

Dear God, thank You for friendships that are loyal and true. Help us to be faithful to our friends and family. Amen.

A Simple Prayer

This month, we are learning to trust God and receive His peace.

When King Saul was trying to kill David, Jonathan brought his friend peace by helping him escape to safety. By doing what is right, we receive the peace that only God can give us. When we do what pleases God, He fills us with peace and we can share that provision with others, just like Jonathan brought greater peace to David.

During April, pray this simple prayer with your family, thanking God for His peace in you!

Jesus, You are the Prince of peace. Thank You for giving us courage in place of fear, confidence in place of insecurity, and peace in place of worry. Teach us to cultivate peace in our lives and in our relationships with one another. Help us to grow and serve you always. Amen.

Bible Verse of the Week

"A friend is always loyal, and a brother is born to help in time of need" (Proverbs 17:17; NLT).

One of the best ways to grow personally and as a family is to memorize Scripture.

This week, we learned how Jonathan helped David. We witnessed God's provision as David escaped to safety.

Take the time to memorize Proverbs 17:17 with your family! Write it out and post it to your refrigerator. Let each person in your family have the opportunity to say it aloud, and then say it all together. Have fun enjoying the Word of God as a family!

Dear God, thank You for the Bible. Help us to memorize Your Word and to hide it in our hearts. Amen.

April 26
Do it!

Sometimes, we can go about our daily lives while forgetting to tell the people we care about just how much we love them. It's always a good reminder to affirm our friends and family. It shows them we care and that we see and value them.

Take the time today to go out of your way to encourage or validate someone you love. Write them a card or make a phone call; send an email, or give them a hug. By doing so, you show care for your friends. Just like Jonathan and David were best friends, you can be a best friend to someone, too! Being loyal and doing what is right can create the lasting type of relationships that God honors.

Dear God, help me to be a loyal and kind friend who is good to others. Give me eyes to see my friends rightly and give me words to encourage them. Amen.

Talk About It

Do you have a best friend? It could be a sibling, a neighbor down the street or at school, or even a pet!

Take a few minutes to share with your family about your best friend. Tell each other what you like and appreciate about your best friend. Brainstorm and share ways you can be a good and supportive friend. Make sure to encourage and reach out to your friends often and let them know that you care about them.

Dear God, thank You for friends! Help me to purposefully care and reach out to my friends, showing them love like You show me. Amen.

April 28

Serve One Another

Sometimes, friends need our help! If you've ever had family friends who have welcomed a new baby or gone through a tough time, you may have made a meal for them or helped out in some other way. Bringing comfort and practical care when a friend is going through a difficult time is a great way to show them you love them!

Find a friend who might need something right now. Whether it's a meal, an encouraging word, or a ride to or from an event, be a true friend—someone who offers needed help. Doing so helps us live the way Jesus lived. It also helps us flourish in the type of community to which God calls us!

Dear God, remind me to look out for the needs of my friends. Help me to bring comfort and practical care to those who need it. Amen.

April 29

Eat Together

Life is better with a little comfort food! Some recipes bring warmth and a kind of contented peace to the heart. Macaroni and cheese may be a familiar dish that you love. It is warm, soft, and flavorful, and known for being a family favorite, especially among kids!

Take the opportunity today to cook up some mac and cheese. It can be a homemade recipe or from a box. Either way, this well-loved dish can remind you of care, comfort, and friendship!. However you choose to make your mac and cheese, it will be even better if you add parmesan cheese on top, and eat it while it's warm and fresh from the stovetop or oven.

While sharing this comfort food, share with your family your favorite part of this week's story about Jonathan and David. What surprised you or delighted you about their friendship?

Dear God, thank You for shared meals and food that comforts us. Help us to bring comfort and care to one another. Amen.

April 30

A King After God's Own Heart
1 Samuel 16–2 Samuel 2

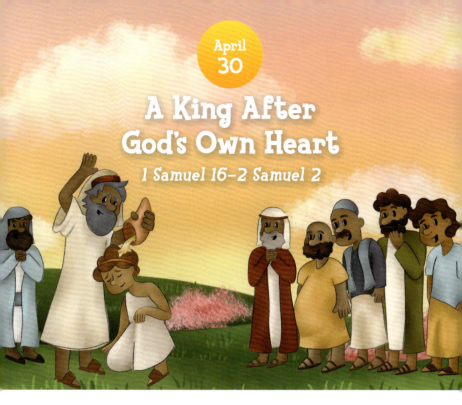

Years passed after David had to run from King Saul. God had been with David as he fought Goliath, fought battles, escaped King Saul, and led the Israelite army. Now,

King Saul and three of his sons died in war. Unfortunately, Jonathan was one of them. David grieved the loss of his friend, but he also knew it was time for him to become king. God was with him as David led the people. He made mistakes, but He loved God, and God also brought him success.

Dear God, we celebrate the fact that You have good plans for us, just as you did for David. Help us to serve You wholeheartedly and with passion. Amen.

A Simple Prayer

This month we are learning to live fully for God and receive His joy. David was called "a man after God's own heart" because he truly loved God and wanted to please Him. He worshiped God wholeheartedly. By worshiping the Lord even when we fail and make mistakes, we receive the fullness of joy that only God can provide for us.

During May, pray this simple prayer with your family, thanking God for His joy in you!

Jesus, we are so grateful that our joy is made full in Your presence. Thank you for this fruit of the Spirit. Teach us how to cultivate joy in our lives and in our relationships with one another. Help us to grow and serve you always. Amen.

Bible Verse of the Week

"You saw me before I was born. Every day of my life was recorded in your book. Every moment was laid out before a single day had passed" (Psalm 139:16; NLT).

One of the best ways to grow personally and as a family is to memorize Scripture.

This week, we learned how David became king. We witnessed God's plan as David was promoted in God's time.

Take the time to memorize Psalm 139:16 with your family! Write it out and post it to your refrigerator. Let each person in your family have the opportunity to say it aloud, and then say it all together. Have fun enjoying the Word of God as a family!

Dear God, thank You for the Bible. Help us to memorize Your Word and to hide it in our hearts. Amen.

May 3

Do it!

Have you ever had a dream of doing something as big as what David? Maybe you don't dream of being king of a country someday; but do you have any other hopes or goals you'd like to accomplish? God loves it when we dream with Him to do good works that help others come to know Jesus and live healthy lives.

Sit down and write out some hopes and dreams for yourself and for your family. Write out one of David's psalms to encourage yourself in the Lord. Pray for God's plan to be done in your life as you listen and try to follow Him. When you have a tough day, and things don't seem to be going so well, take out the psalm and read it over yourself.

Stand tall, say a prayer out loud, and ask God for the strength to do His will. Prayer changes things!

Dear God, thank You for strengthening us in the Lord by David's example. Help us to lean on You and speak your truth. Amen.

Talk About It

A really fun and interesting way to grow and learn is to ask your parents to tell you some of their stories! Take the opportunity today to ask your parents or grandparents about their childhood. Ask them what did they wanted to be when they grew up. Did it happen? Did they have any thoughts or plans for their future? How did God show up in their lives and direct their paths? Hearing these stories helps families understand who their parents and grandparents are and where they come from. It also brings wisdom. We often learn best when someone tells us how they succeeded and how they failed . . . and how God taught them lessons in the middle of all of it!

Take this opportunity to learn from the elders in your life and grow in your faith and joy.

Dear God, thank You for older people in my life who have stories to tell. Help me to listen and grow by their wisdom. Amen.

May 5

Serve One Another

King David did many good things. He was known as a man after God's heart. He was a worshiper and musician. He was also a soldier who fought many wars. He prayed and wrote many psalms, also known as songs. He loved God with a lot of passion. Sometimes his passion was geared toward other things and got him into trouble.

Do you know anyone who has a lot of energy? Does the person you know ever get in trouble because they might get hyper? Do they ever need to find new outlets for their actions? It's good to have a lot of passion, and it's also good to know how to focus that energy on something that is helpful.

Who in your life has a lot of passion? Is it you? A sibling? Make a list of a few things you can do when you or your passionate friend need to be redirected or focused on the right path. Perhaps you can pray, be honest with yourself or your friend, find reminders in Scripture of the right things to do, or even calm yourself or your friend. Honoring God with passion is good, and honoring God with obedience is also great! Misplaced passion can cause us a lot of trouble.

Dear God, help me to use my passion for Your good. Help me to be a good friend to others who have a passion for Your Kingdom, as well. Amen.

May 6
Eat Together

A coronation is the ceremony in which a king or queen is proclaimed a royal. Most often, an elaborate party follows a coronation.

Coronation parties are filled with all kinds of fun foods! Have a small coronation party to celebrate the life of King David. Set out small teacups for different flavors of hot tea. Make several different sandwiches using your choice of meats or cheeses; then cut each sandwich into four triangular pieces. By enjoying these special snacks, you can eat like a king or queen! If you're still hungry, you can add fruit at the end!

Take the moments while you enjoy your sandwiches and tea to talk about what you learned this week. What stood out to you about David's story? How can you relate to him? How can you thank God for what He did for David? What might God do for you?

Dear God, You are a good God filled with joy. Thank You for letting us rejoice in You through David's psalms. Amen.

The Wise King
1 Kings 3

After King David ruled Israel for forty years, his son, Solomon, became the next king. God spoke to Solomon one night in a dream. He told Solomon that whatever he asked for would be given to him.

Thankfully, Solomon asked for something good! He asked God to give him wisdom so he could lead the people of Israel well. God not only gave him wisdom, but He also gave him riches and fame.

Because Solomon was so wise, people came to him when they needed someone to settle arguments and disputes. One day, two women who were arguing about a baby came to him. Both women claimed to be the child's mother. Solomon heard the stories of both women, then he said they should cut the baby in half, and each of them could have half of the baby. One woman said that was fine, and the other woman said "No! Don't kill the baby. Let her have it, so it can live." Solomon then knew that the second woman, the one who would give up her child rather than see it killed, was the real mother. What a wise man!

Dear God, thank You for Your wisdom. Help us to seek You and wisdom throughout the days of our lives. Amen.

A Simple Prayer

This month, we are learning to ask for wisdom and receive God's joy.

When Solomon became king, he requested wisdom from God. His request was granted and he was used by God to lead the people well. Solomon and the people of Israel lived lives of contentment; following the path of God's wisdom increased their joy. By employing God's wisdom God's way, we receive the fullness of joy that only God can provide for us.

During May, pray this simple prayer with your family, thanking God for His joy in you!

Jesus, we are so grateful that our joy is made full in Your presence. Thank you for this fruit of the Spirit. Teach us how to cultivate joy in our lives and in our relationships with one another. Help us to grow and serve you always. Amen.

May 9

Bible Verse of the Week

"How much better to get wisdom than gold, and good judgment than silver!" (Proverbs 16:16; NLT).

One of the best ways to grow personally and as a family is to memorize Scripture.

This week, we learned that Solomon became king of Israel. We learned how He asked for God's wisdom to lead the people of Israel well.

Take the time to memorize Proverbs 16:16 with your family! Write it out and post it to your refrigerator. Let each person in your family have the opportunity to say it aloud, and then say it all together. Have fun enjoying the Word of God as a family!

Dear God, thank You for the Bible. Help us to memorize Your Word and to hide it in our hearts. Amen.

May 10

Do it!

We can ask God for wisdom, but we must decide to put that wisdom into practice! Think through your decisions very carefully today. Make it a priority to ask God for wisdom to make the best choice; then do as He leads.

If you have homework to do, should you do it right away or procrastinate? If the toilet paper roll is left empty, should you leave it empty or replace it? If you have ice cream for dessert, should you have one scoop or two?

These may seem like small things, but the more you seek wisdom in the small things, the more you'll be prepared for the big decisions. As we take the step to listen to God, we must also pay attention to what He says. We should focus more on what we need, instead of mostly on what we want. When our priorities are right, we will be able to hear Him much better. When we hear God well, it's easier to do good and to experience joy.

Dear God, You are full of wisdom, self-control, and joy. Help us to listen for Your voice and follow through on Your leading. Amen.

Talk About It

It's pretty amazing to think that Solomon could have asked God for anything he wanted. Can you imagine? There are a lot of things we could ask for: money, power, fame, happiness. The list could go on and on.

But Solomon didn't ask for any of those things! He asked for wisdom to lead God's people well; and God provided just that . . . and more.

Take this opportunity to talk with your family about what you might like to ask God for and why. Listen to your family members' answers and talk through the details. Take this opportunity to hear the hearts of those you love and respond to them with heart-felt truth in return.

Dear God, You give good gifts, not only to benefit us, but for us to benefit others. Help us to be good stewards of those gifts. Amen.

May 12

Serve One Another

Serving one another can occur in a lot of different ways. This week, we learned about Solomon's request for wisdom.

Take time today to sit quietly and pray for God to give you wisdom. Then, take out three notecards; on the top of one write "helpful," on another, write "wise," and on the third, write "kind." Throughout the day, keep track of whatever choices you made that were helpful, wise, or kind. Record the good you did, and ask God to continue to expand your opportunities to do good with joy in your heart. At the end of the day, give your card to your mom or dad. Ask them to use it as a bookmark in their Bible! They will love the encouragement, and they can celebrate with you.

Dear God, help us to serve one another with kindness and wisdom. Remind us to encourage each other with our prayers and actions. Amen.

May 13

Eat Together

Time to make a salty and sweet treat!

Get two plates from your kitchen and go through the cupboards to find both salty and sweet foods. Your salty foods go on one plate (these can include meat, nuts, and other salty snacks). On the second plate, put your sweet foods like cookies, candies, or fruit of some kind.

Sit both plates in the center of the table and take turns with your family members picking a salty food and a sweet food. Think of the salty foods as wisdom, and the sweet foods as celebration. It's good to have a balance of both! As you taste each of the foods, talk through this week's lesson about Solomon and name ways he walked with wisdom.

Dear God, thank You for teaching us about wisdom and joy this week. Help us to live according to Your plans and goodwill. Amen.

The One True God
1 Kings 18

May 14

At the end of Solomon's reign, a new king of Israel was set in place. His name was Ahab. King Ahab worshiped a false god named Baal, even though he knew the first commandment from Moses was to worship no other gods but the one true God. Ahab didn't listen. His disobedience caused a horrible drought. Because of Ahab's disobedience, God sent a prophet named Elijah to challenge Ahab to a competition. Elijah would pray to the real God, and Ahab would have 450 of his men pray to Baal. The true God would answer with fire. Ahab agreed and built an altar, and his 450 false priests called on the name of Baal. Nothing happened.

Elijah then built an altar to the true God, and he even heavily soaked it with water. When Elijah called on the Lord, fire struck from heaven and completely burned up the altar (even the stones) and dried up all the water! When Ahab and his men saw this, they immediately fell to the ground and realized the Lord is the true God. Shortly thereafter, God ended the drought and a heavy rain soaked the dry ground.

Dear God, thank You for being the one true God. Help us to worship You only. Amen.

A Simple Prayer

This month, we are worshiping the one true God, the only God in whom joy is found.

When Elijah was sent to challenge King Ahab and the false god, Baal, our one true God revealed Himself with fire. Only He has power over even the wind and rain. We receive the fullness of joy when we worship the Lord, and only the one true God can provide that for us.

During May, pray this simple prayer with your family, thanking God for His joy in you!

Jesus, we are so grateful that our joy is made full in Your presence. Thank you for this fruit of the Spirit. Teach us how to cultivate joy in our lives and in our relationships with one another. Help us to grow and serve you always. Amen.

May 16

Bible Verse of the Week

One of the best ways to grow personally and as a family is to memorize Scripture.

This week, we learned how Elijah was sent by God. We learned how Elijah called on the name of the one true God, and how the Lord answered with fire, proving Himself to be the only God!

Take the time to memorize 1 Chronicles 29:11 with your family! Write it out and post it to your refrigerator. Let each person in your family have the opportunity to say it aloud, and then say it all together. Have fun enjoying the Word of God as a family!

Dear God, thank You for the Bible. Help us to memorize Your Word and to hide it in our hearts. Amen.

"Yours, O Lord, is the greatness, the power, the glory, the victory, and the majesty. Everything in the heavens and on the earth is yours, O Lord, and this is your kingdom. We adore you as the one who is over all things" (1 Chronicles 29:11; NLT).

May 17

Do it!

This week, we've been learning about Elijah calling on the name of the one true God, and God answering with fire! Amazingly, even though Elijah saturated the altar with buckets of water, it still caught fire; everything, including the stones were completely burned up because the Lord was behind it. This teaches us that we can trust God. When we follow Him faithfully, listen to Him closely, and worship only Him, He will prove Himself strong.

Go outside to your backyard this evening with your family members. Ask an adult to build a campfire in a safe area, like a fire pit. Watch it as it grows. What do you observe about the fire? How does it smell? How does it make you feel when watching it? If you don't have a fire pit in your backyard, consider your indoor fireplace or a candle. Wherever you would like to build a fire, get your parents' permission first!

Talk about Elijah's story and discuss what it taught you about God.

Dear God, thank You for saving us, providing for us, and teaching us about Your holiness. Help us to listen to You. Amen.

May 18

Talk About It

This week, we learned that Elijah was brave as he confronted Ahab, his men, and Baal. He needed God's presence to increase his courage and lead his every action.

Have you ever had to be brave like Elijah?

Think about school or sports. Has a friend or teammate ever tried to get you to do something wrong or unkind? How did you respond? Sometimes it takes courage to speak up for ourselves. Did you end up doing the right thing or the wrong thing? If you did the right thing, what happened? If you did the wrong thing, what happened?

Set aside a few minutes today to talk with your family about what happens and how it feels when we do something right versus when we do something we know is wrong. Pray together and ask God to help you choose what is right.

Dear God, please give us your wisdom from Heaven. We need help to do what is right. Amen.

May 19

Serve One Another

Before we act, it's always a good idea to pray. Prayer connects us with God. Through prayer, we repent, praise, and worship Jesus. By prayer, we can ask God to stop bad things from happening, we can ask Him to protect others, and we can request that He encourage those who need it.

No matter our circumstances, we can always pray and ask Jesus to show Himself to our family, friends, and loved ones. When we pray that God would meet us in our needs and in our hurts, we can shift the atmosphere from the worship the world's ungodly values into worship of almighty God.

Ask God to give you the name of a one loved one you can pray for today. Set aside time a few minutes to lift them in prayer today.

Dear God, thank You for my friends. Please touch them with Your presence, show them they are loved, and help them to turn away from any ungodly worldly values. Amen.

Eat Together

This week we learned about fire from heaven. You know what goes great with fire? S'mores!

Gather a bag of marshmallows, a few chocolate bars, and a box of graham crackers. If the weather allows, consider an outdoor S'mores party. Simply heat the marshmallow on a long stick over the fire. Grab two graham crackers and set one chocolate on one of them. When the marshmallow is melted, smoosh it between the grahams and chocolate. If you don't have a campfire, you can heat the marshmallows for a few seconds in the microwave! Keep a close eye on your marshmallows, as it does not take long for them to burn.

Take a few minutes to enjoy this treat as a family, relishing the sweetness and letting it remind you of the sweet victory found in the one true God.

Dear God, You are the winner! Help us stand in victory with You while experiencing the fullness of Your joy! Amen.

May 21

Elisha, the Prophet's Apprentice
1 Kings 19–2 Kings 2,4

We are told of twelve miracles performed by Elijah, including calling down fire from heaven, raising the dead, and causing a drought. After serving God and man for many decades, God called Elijah to heaven. He had an assistant named Elisha, and Elisha asked Elijah for double his spirit as well as to help people twice as much as Elijah had. God responded to Elisha's prayer, and he went on to do sixteen miracles because he had a heart to help others.

During Elisha's ministry, he performed sixteen miracles, including cleansing a bowl of water with salt to make it pure, helping a poor widow by miraculously multiplying cooking oil, and bringing a dead boy back to life! Because of his heart to serve, God gave Elisha opportunities to do just that.

Dear God, thank You for teaching us about Elisha's heart to serve. Help us to experience Your fullness as we help others, too. Amen.

May 22

A Simple Prayer

This month, we are learning about the joy of the Lord.

When Elijah went into heaven, Elisha's desire was to serve others by following in Elijah's footsteps. Elisha asked God for double the anointing Elijah had so that he could help bring joy and healing to those who needed it. He had a heart to serve, and serving others is a wonderful way to find and express God's joy.

During May, pray this simple prayer with your family, thanking God for His joy in you!

Jesus, we are so grateful that our joy is made full in Your presence. Thank you for this fruit of the Spirit. Teach us how to cultivate joy in our lives and in our relationships with one another. Help us to grow and serve you always. Amen.

May 23

Bible Verse of the Week

One of the best ways to grow personally and as a family is to memorize Scripture.

We learned how Elisha followed in Elijah's footsteps. Just as He did when working through Elijah, when Elisha helped others, God provided the miraculous.

Take the time to memorize Matthew 7:8 with your family! Write it out and post it to your refrigerator. Let each person in your family have the opportunity to say it aloud, and then say it all together. Have fun enjoying the Word of God as a family!

Dear God, thank You for the Bible. Help us to memorize Your Word and to hide it in our hearts. Amen.

"For anyone who asks, receives. Everyone who seeks, finds. And to everyone who knocks, the door will be opened" (Matthew 7:8; NLT).

May 24

Do it!

Have you ever wanted to serve God and others so much that you spent time in prayer asking God for the ability to do so? Elisha teaches us a very important lesson: God answers our prayers. Elisha prayed and received what he asked God for. Sometimes, though, God answers us in a way that seems different than what we hoped. When that happens, it's important to wait and keep listening for God's solution. Sometimes, there's a good reason for God to delay; sometimes, God has something better in mind for us.

Get out a piece of paper and a pencil. Make two lists; one list should be five or six prayers you've prayed, and the other list should be the answers God gave you for each prayer. Look through the lists, and celebrate the ways God answered your prayers, whether the answers were what you expected or not!

Dear God, thank You for hearing us. Help us to pray often and to receive Your answers. Amen.

Talk About It

Elisha likely experienced God's joy in a special way as he served others through prayer and miracles.

What's your favorite way to help others in big or small ways? How does serving others make you feel?

Sit around the table with your family and take a few minutes to talk about the ways that you love to serve other people. Tell a few stories about when you helped someone and what happened in the process. Celebrate and thank God for the opportunity to be part of His ministry on earth.

Dear God, it's a gift to be able to serve You and others. Thank You for filling our hearts as we honor You and those around us. Amen.

May 26

Serve One Another

It is likely a beautiful day in May where you are! Take this opportunity to make some fresh lemonade or a drink of your choice and then host a beverage stand in your neighborhood for an hour or two. Giving someone a cool drink brings them and you refreshment and encouragement!

After you have collected your earnings, donate the money to your church on Sunday. Ask God to take the little you gave and multiply it to be double the impact! This is exactly what was in Elisha's heart when he asked for a double portion of Elijah's God-given ability.

Be encouraged that little things matter, and you can serve others right where you are.

Dear God, help us to serve You in big and small ways. Guide us to opportunities to make the world a better place. Amen.

May 27

Eat Together

Let's take the opportunity to eat together today! Think of a few snacks that are better when they contain twice the goodness. Maybe you prefer a double-stuffed Oreo™? Maybe you would like a sandwich with peanut butter and jelly? What are a few things in your kitchen or pantry that already have two layers? If you can't find anything you love, consider a short trip to the grocery store to look for items that are double in some way.

Even in the simple situations of everyday life, we can be like Elisha and bless those around us with twice as much of the goodness and love of God than we ever thought we could.

Dear God, thank You for Your never-ending love for us. Help us to receive from You and give to others. Amen.

The Girl Who Saved Her People
Esther 1–10

After the days of Elijah and Elisha, there was a Persian king named Xerxes. He was used to telling people what to do, so when his wife wouldn't obey him, he got angry and made her leave. He decided to hold a beauty contest to find a new queen.

As soon as he saw an absolutely gorgeous girl named Esther, he chose her to be the next queen. Esther was a Jewish orphan. Unfortunately, one of the king's advisors, named Haman, wanted all the Jews in Persia to die! Esther's cousin, Mordecai, found out about Haman's evil plan. He encouraged Esther to go to the king and tell him about the awful plan in order to save her people. He said to her: "Perhaps God made you queen for such a time as this?"

No one went to the king uninvited; doing so could mean death. But Esther bravely appeared before him. King Xerxes responded favorably and listened to her. When Xerxes learned of Haman's evil plot, he sent Haman to be killed and gave Mordecai his role. Esther saved her people!

Dear God, thank You for the courage to do what is right. Help us to follow in Esther's brave footsteps, knowing we were also made for such a time as this. Amen.

May 29

A Simple Prayer

This month, we are learning about the joy of living for God. When Esther went to see the king without an invitation, she could have been filled with fear. Instead, she chose to lean on the joy of the Lord. Without God, she would have been too fearful to risk her life to save her people. Esther's beauty was deep; she had a beautiful heart to do what was right.

May we also choose to lean into the Lord when faced with difficult things. This brings about deep joy in our hearts.

During May, pray this simple prayer with your family, thanking God for His joy in you!

Jesus, we are so grateful that our joy is made full in Your presence. Thank you for this fruit of the Spirit. Teach us how to cultivate you in our lives and in our relationships with one another. Help us to grow and serve you always. Amen.

May 30

Bible Verse of the Week

"If you keep quiet at a time like this, deliverance and relief for the Jews will arise from some other place, but you and your relatives will die. Who knows if perhaps you were made queen for such a time as this?" (Esther 4:14, NLT).

One of the best ways to grow personally and as a family is to memorize Scripture.

This week, we learned how Esther saved her people. Esther came fearlessly before the king unannounced and bravely spoke the truth!

Take the time to memorize Esther 4:14 with your family! Write it out and post it to your refrigerator. Let each person in your family have the opportunity to say it aloud, and then say it all together. Have fun enjoying the Word of God as a family!

Dear God, thank You for the Bible. Help us to memorize Your Word and to hide it in our hearts. Amen.

May 31

Do it!

We must lean on God to find the courage to do what is right! Two of the best ways are to pray and to read the Bible. We can know what is right, good, and true by knowing God and His Word.

Take the opportunity to go to the Scriptures about Esther today. You don't have to read the entire book, but there are only ten chapters and it's a great story. Pray to Jesus before reading your Bible, asking Him to teach you to understand the Scriptures the way He intends; then read the story of Esther.

What did you learn? Were there any details that stuck out to you? Write them down. You can talk as a family about what you learned, or you can research to learn more!

Dear God, You are so good and faithful to provide Your Word for us. Help us to pray and read it with an eager and joyful heart. Amen.

Talk About it!

Esther had a difficult job to do, didn't she? Have you ever had to do something that required courage? Speaking up when others are doing wrong can take bravery, but it is the right thing to do.

Think about a time or situation in which someone you know was not being treated right. They may have been bullied at school, picked on by a sibling, or treated badly by a neighbor. Did you say anything? If you did, how did it go? If you didn't, what happened?

Talk with your family about some ways you might be able to support someone who is being mistreated. There are a lot of bullies in life, but God is stronger and smarter. He will always show us how to come to the aid of those who are mistreated and love them well.

Dear God, please give us wisdom on how to care for others who need it. Show us how to speak up and be kind. Amen.

June 2

Serve One Another

After King Xerxes chose her, Esther had to prepare to be the Queen. She purified her body through special baths over a period of months before she actually became Queen. Just like Esther had to prepare to serve, we should also prepare our lives to serve others.

Have you ever realized that it's difficult to invite others to your home when your room or house is messy? Failing to upkeep your room can actually result in a loss of motivation. A room that is uninviting can also make you less effective as a friend than if you had your room ready to accept guests.

Take the time today to do a room or home clean-up! Organize and prepare your home so that you are ready to accept opportunities to serve. When our lives are in good shape, we have room to help others without feeling stressed out. By cleaning your own space, you will have the desire and motivation to help someone else!

Dear God, remind us to stay organized and focused so we can serve You better. By doing so, we give others a better gift of love. Amen.

June 3

Eat Together

Esther went through her baths and purifying rituals; it is likely that she also ate a good diet.

Keeping our bodies healthy is a wonderful way to serve God and remain active in our lives.

Take this opportunity to make a smoothie full of your favorite fruits and vegetables. You can choose any combination of spinach, kale, pineapple, apples, strawberries . . . whatever fruits and vegetables you prefer. You may even want to include a little bit of plain yogurt or protein powder. Add a little ice if your fruit is not already frozen.

While having your smoothie, thank God for your health! By fueling our bodies with what is good for us, we can serve God and others better.

Dear God, thank You for our health! Thank You for healthy foods to eat so that we can be nourished and ready to serve you and others. Amen.

June 4
Three Friends in the Hot Seat
Daniel 3

Prior to the time of Esther, a Babylonian king named Nebuchadnezzar ruled the Israelites. Nebuchadnezzar had a giant statue of himself made and demanded that everyone to bow down and worship it. Moses had told the Israelites not to bow to idols or worship anything but the one true God, so they all struggled with the rule. Three of the Israelites refused to bow down to the idol. Their names were Shadrach, Meshach, and Abednego.

This made the king very angry, and he commanded that the three friends be thrown into a fiery furnace. They still refused to bow to the statue, and the king ordered guards to throw them into the flames. It was so hot that the guards died, but Shadrach, Meshach, and Abednego were not harmed! They were seen walking around inside the flames with a fourth, unknown figure. They eventually came out of the furnace completely untouched. They didn't even smell like smoke.

Even King Nebuchadnezzar realized God had sent an angel to rescue the men. He and all the people praised God.

Dear God, it can sometimes be difficult to do the right thing. Help us to be brave like Shadrach, Meshach, and Abednego. Amen.

June 5

A Simple Prayer

This month, we are learning about the goodness of God. When Shadrach, Meshach, and Abednego refused to bow down to the idol, they knew that even if they perished, worshiping God only was the right thing to do. God showed His goodness by sending His angel to be with them in the furnace.

During June, pray this simple prayer with your family, thanking God for His goodness over you!

Jesus, we are so grateful that goodness is a gift from You. Thank you for helping us help others as we fully rely on You. Teach us how to receive and cultivate goodness in our lives and in our relationships with one another. Help us to grow and serve you always. Amen.

June 6

Bible Verse of the Week

One of the best ways to grow personally and as a family is to memorize Scripture.

Today, we learned how Shadrach, Meshach, and Abednego worshiped God, even when they were threatened by death in a fiery furnace. God provided for them; even their enemies praised God.

Take the time to memorize Romans 1:16 with your family! Write it out and post it to your refrigerator. Let each person in your family have the opportunity to say it aloud, and then say it all together. Have fun enjoying the Word of God as a family!

Dear God, thank You for the Bible. Help us to memorize Your Word and to hide it in our hearts. Amen.

> "For I am not ashamed of this Good News about Christ. It is the power of God at work, saving everyone who believes—the Jew first and also the Gentile"" (Romans 1:16; NLT).

June 7

Do it!

When we choose to do what is right, God always comes through for us, even though we might not see it right away. He is always faithful to us. Can you think of a time when you chose to do right in the eyes of God even though everyone around you was doing the wrong thing?

Do some role playing with your family today. Pick a scenario in which the choices are clearly either right in the eyes of God or completely wrong. Once you have chosen, make your case for doing the right thing while the rest of your family argues against your choice. Stand your ground! By simply acting this out, you will gain strength and courage for a time when you may need it. Give everyone in your family a turn to choose a scenario. Once all have had a turn at standing on the side of right, spend time celebrating God's leading in our lives and thank Him in prayer.

Dear God, thank You for helping us do what is right! You are the best! And we worship only You. Amen.

June 8
Talk About It

Have you ever been afraid of something, big or small? What was it? Describe the fear you felt with a few adjectives. What caused your fear?

This week, sit with your family and let everyone share about a fear he or she has battled. Just sharing what scares us can often lessen fear's power in our lives. Honest conversation about specific fears will bring opportunities to pray for one another. Locate a few Bible verses that address how God helps us overcome fear and pray for all your family's fears to be dismantled by Jesus. Encourage each other to keep being brave!

Dear God, we give You our fears. Help us to release what hinders us from worshiping You completely. Amen.

June 9

Serve One Another

Consider the fears you discussed with your family yesterday. Are there situations you fear while other family members have faith to withstand them? Do you have faith to endure something that someone else in your family fears?

Take the opportunity to support and encourage your family members in the areas your faith is strong. Then, be willing to accept encouragement from family members who have faith in areas where you are fearful. Are there any baby steps toward faith you can take today to begin walking out of fear? Are there any areas where you can repent and ask God to heal your fear?

By helping to boost the faith of family members, you are serving each other. Take a few baby steps toward a faithful heart today.

Dear God, help us to be faithful, knowing that You are good. Please give us encouragement when we still struggle with fear. Amen.

June 10

Eat Together

Faith is like a structure, built layer by layer. Each layer may require facing fear. But purposing to operate in trust of God each step of the way will result in a strong and sure faith.

Since it's a summer day, take this opportunity to layer up your favorite burger from the grill or stovetop. Season up your favorite beef or turkey, form burgers and grill them to your liking. Then consciously add one layer at a time of cheese, lettuce, tomato, onion, ketchup, mustard—whatever you prefer. As each layer is added, thank God aloud for giving you faith for the next step in life. That first delicious bite can remind you that once the work is done, you can enjoy the resulting strong faith.

Enjoy sharing what you learned about the Shadrach, Meshach, and Abednego this week with your family.

Dear God, thank You for faith that nourishes our souls. Help us to remember to thank You often for Your goodness and faithfulness. Amen.

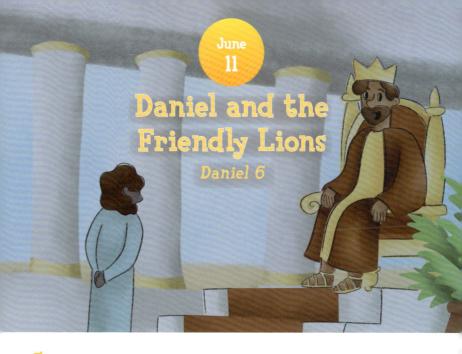

Daniel and the Friendly Lions

Daniel 6

June 11

Shadrach, Meshach, and Abednego had a friend named Daniel. They all had jobs, and Daniel was very good at his. He was so good that the new King Darius and his advisors were jealous of him. They even wanted to get rid of him. Because they knew that Daniel only prayed to the true God, they decided to make a law forcing everyone to pray to the king. When Daniel refused, the king had him thrown in a lion's den. They thought their plan had worked, but the King liked Daniel and went to check on him.

When he got there, Daniel was just fine because God had protected him. God had shut the mouths of the lions. The King was astonished and so angry at his advisors that he sent them to the lions' den instead.

Dear God, thank You for helping us choose what is right, no matter the circumstances. And thank You for always protecting us. Amen.

A Simple Prayer

This month, we are learning about the goodness of God.

When Daniel was thrown into the lion's den, he should have been killed. But God protected Daniel. God showed His goodness by closing the mouths of the lions.

During June, pray this simple prayer with your family, thanking God for His goodness over you!

Jesus, we are so grateful that goodness is a gift from You. Thank you for helping us help others as we fully rely on You. Teach us how to receive and cultivate goodness in our lives and in our relationships with one another. Help us to grow and serve you always. Amen.

June 13

Bible Verse of the Week

"O Sovereign LORD! You made the heavens and earth by your strong hand and powerful arm. Nothing is too hard for you" (Jeremiah 32:1;7 NLT).

One of the best ways to grow personally and as a family is to memorize Scripture.

Today, we learned how Daniel was protected when thrown into the lion's den. He did the right thing by refusing to pray to the king and praying only to God. God proved His goodness when He spared Daniel's life.

Take the time to memorize Jeremiah 32:17 with your family! Write it out and post it to your refrigerator. Let each member of your family have the opportunity to say it aloud, and then say it all together. Have fun enjoying the Word of God as a family!

Dear God, thank You for the Bible. Help us to memorize Your Word and to hide it in our hearts. Amen.

June 14
Do it!

Have you ever seen a lion up close? If you can, take advantage of the summer weather and take a trip to the zoo sometime this week. See if you can observe a lion.

What would it feel like to be thrown into a group of these hungry beasts? Observe how big the lions are, how powerful their paws look, and how vicious looking their teeth are. How much do you think they weigh?

All of these details give us a small glimpse of what Daniel likely saw and experienced when he was thrown into the lion's den. Knowing God was protecting him while there must have been an amazing experience! I'm sure he was praising God for His goodness by shutting the mouths of the lions.

Dear God, You are worthy to be praised! You are good and protect us with Your mighty hand. Amen.

June 15

Talk About It

God's protection can be experienced in a lot of different ways. Sometimes His protection is obvious and other times He works behind-the-scenes. Perhaps God has protected you in an obvious way by preventing a car accident or stopping a fire, but perhaps he also has intervened without you knowing it.

Have a conversation with your family today about the ways you know God has preserved you. Maybe you haven't been in a den with lions, but we all have known times where God's hand has protected our lives. Thank Him for it and be sure to celebrate His goodness.

Dear God, thank You for the many times You have protected us, whether we knew it or not. Your love for us saves us. Amen.

June 16

Serve One Another

In this week's story about Daniel, we saw how the advisors to the king tried to set Daniel up. They purposefully made the law that all citizens had to pray to the king because they knew Daniel wouldn't oblige. He continued praying to God, no matter what.

Have you ever been in a situation in which someone tried to set you up to be hurt or harmed? It doesn't feel good, does it? Let's practice doing the opposite this week by serving one another. Take the opportunity to "outdo one another in honor" (Romans 12:10) by intentionally doing a kind deed for the people or pets in your home. You can decide how you'd like to serve, whether you do the dishes for your mom, or take the dog for a walk, clean up the garage for your dad, or write an encouraging note to a sibling. The possibilities are endless! Whatever you do, do it for the good of someone you love!

Dear God, help me to remember to honor others in all things. Give me the grace and strength to esteem others more than myself. Amen.

June 17

Eat Together

Let's share some breakfast together! You'll need:

Frozen waffles (or make your own in the waffle maker)

2 or 3 oranges

Blueberries

Strawberries

Butter or syrup to your liking

Place your waffles in the toaster, and heat to your liking. While your waffles are browning, peel your orange and separate it into slices. After you take out the waffles, butter them to taste. Place the sliced oranges around the outside of the waffle like a lion's mane. Put two blueberries in the center of the waffle for eyes and slice the strawberry for a snout. Drizzle syrup to your liking and enjoy devouring your lion!

Celebrate God's goodness this week as you recall the things you learned about Daniel.

Dear God, You are the best! Thank You for Your goodness and for protecting us every day. Amen.

Jonah and the Great Fish
Jonah 1-4

June 18

Jonah was a prophet in Israel. Nineveh, an enemy of Israel, was a pagan city over 500 miles away. God asked Jonah to tell the people of Nineveh to stop doing wrong. God wanted the people to stop worshiping idols. If they did not, He planned to destroy their city.

Jonah didn't want to share God's message with Nineveh. He hated Ninevites and hoped their land would be destroyed. If he refused to go, they would never hear God's message, they would not repent, and they would cease to exist. To avoid obeying the Lord, Johah hopped on a ship to sail far away from Nineveh. God sent a storm that threatened to rip the ship apart. Jonah knew the storm was sent because of his disobedience. When the ship's crew found out, Jonah was thrown overboard. It was not long before Johah was swallowed whole by a huge fish! Jonah prayed to God while he was inside the fish. The fish spat him out three days later, and Jonah went to Nineveh immediately to preach God's message. He told them to stop doing evil and to follow God, and they did! God took pity on them and didn't destroy their city.

Dear God, please help us to obey You whenever and whatever You ask! We want to listen and be obedient to You. Amen.

A Simple Prayer

This month, we are learning about the goodness of God.

Jonah initially disobeyed God by ignoring his directions; but God was merciful. He had a huge fish swallow Jonah to give him time to think and pray. Jonah repented and was released by the massive fish to do what he was supposed to. God was good to Jonah and to the people of Nineveh, even when they made mistakes.

During June, pray this simple prayer with your family, thanking God for His goodness over you!

Jesus, we are so grateful that goodness is a gift from You. Thank you for helping us help others as we fully rely on You. Teach us how to receive and cultivate goodness in our lives and in our relationships with one another. Help us to grow and serve you always. Amen.

Bible Verse of the Week

One of the best ways to grow personally and as a family is to memorize Scripture.

This week, we learned how Jonah was sent to speak God's Word to the Ninevites. Even though he ran in the opposite direction at first, God was merciful and changed Jonah's mind.

Take the time to memorize 1 John 1:9 with your family! Write it out and post it to your refrigerator. Let each person in your family have the opportunity to say it aloud, and then say it all together. Have fun enjoying the Word of God as a family!

Dear God, thank You for the Bible. Help us to memorize Your Word and to hide it in our hearts. Amen.

"If we confess our sins, he is faithful and just and will forgive us our sins and purify us from all unrighteousness" (1 John 1:9; NIV).

June 21

Do it!

Have you ever heard the saying "practice makes perfect?" Remembering it can be very helpful when we are practicing showing God's mercy to others. At first, it can feel unfair to have to give mercy to someone who is doing bad things. Jonah was asked to go to Nineveh and didn't want to. Have you ever had to extend mercy to someone when you didn't want to? What did you do?

When we take opportunities to give mercy and goodness to others, it helps us become more like Christ. Mercy becomes easier when we choose to practice it. The more we extend mercy, the easier it becomes. As we learn to see God's mercy in our lives, the more likely we are to share His truth and goodness with others.

Find opportunities this week to look for ways to show love and mercy to others! Share God's truth and love with everyone you meet.

Dear God, help us to practice doing good and showing mercy. We want to love others the way You love us. Amen.

June 22

Talk About It

Spend some time today talking about all the funny and odd details of what you imagine it would be like to be swallowed by a huge fish. Can you imagine the smells, the half-digested food (ewwww!), the darkness, and the fear?

Think of some adjectives that would go along with the experience and share them with your family. Who has the best description? Who has the worst description? A fish's belly would likely be gross, and no one wants to live there for three days!

Thank God He gave you the story of Jonah, so you can learn to listen when God speaks to you. Also, thank God for His mercy and goodness because we often don't listen the first time!

Dear God, thank You for the story of Jonah. Thank You for being faithful to us, even in our sin. You are good. Amen.

June 23

Serve One Another

Today is a great day to show someone mercy! Ask a parent for a household chore you can do, or offer to mow the lawn or take out the trash of a neighbor. Don't ask for payment. Should anyone offer to pay you, take the money and use it to buy a gift for someone else! Show mercy and grace by being generous with your skills and time.

Allow yourself the opportunity to experience all the feelings that mercy and goodness bring. Describe your emotions while choosing to do good and show mercy to others. How did it feel to give away your reward?

Celebrate and praise God for all the ways He shows us His love and goodness.

Dear God, You are merciful and good in all Your ways. Help us to be selfless and loving. Amen.

June 24

Eat Together

Jonah may have thought he was done for when he was swallowed whole by that big fish. And rightly so! It's hard to imagine what it must have been like for him. I wonder if he still enjoyed eating seafood afterward.

What kind of seafood have you experienced? Do you ever eat seafood while on summer vacation? Whether you're at the beach right now or not, take this week to have some type of seafood. You can choose salmon or fish or fish sticks and mac and cheese. If you dislike fish, grab some goldfish crackers. It doesn't have to be complicated, and it doesn't even have to be real seafood (though consider at least giving it a try).

Talk about all you learned from Jonah's story this week and enjoy God's magnificent love poured out as correction and grace.

Dear God, thank You for giving us grace in our weaknesses and correction when we need it. Help us to receive You and Your instructions. Amen.

June 25

Gabriel Visits Mary and Joseph
*Luke 1:26-38;
Matthew 1:18-25*

Nearly 800 years after Jonah's adventures, there was a man named Joseph who was planning to marry a girl named Mary. They lived in Nazareth, a small, humble village in northern Israel. All things seemed normal in their lives, but that was about to change drastically.

One day, Mary was astounded when she was visited by the angel, Gabriel. Gabriel appeared to her and said: "God is pleased with you! Don't be afraid. God has chosen you to give birth to His Son. You will name Him Jesus, and He will reign forever over an endless kingdom."

Mary didn't understand how this could be since she wasn't even married to Joseph, but Gabriel explained to her that "Nothing is impossible with God." Mary believed what the angel told her and surrendered to serve the Lord.

When Joseph heard the news, he thought he should separate himself from Mary quietly, but Gabriel came to him in a dream to explain it all. Joseph chose to believe Gabriel, married Mary, and stood faithfully by her side. They believed God and waited for Jesus to arrive.

Dear God, You are the God of the impossible. Help us to have faith in You like Mary and Joseph did. Amen.

June 26

A Simple Prayer

This month, we are learning about the goodness of God.

The angel, Gabriel, came to visit Mary with really big news. Mary and Joseph both surrendered to the will of God. They continually experienced God's goodness as Mary was blessed to walk out His plan. This remarkable story teaches us that even when favor looks differently than we expect, we can trust Jesus and know God's plan is best.

During June, pray this simple prayer with your family, thanking God for His goodness over you!

Jesus, we are so grateful that goodness is a gift from You. Thank you for helping us help others as we fully rely on You. Teach us how to receive and cultivate goodness in our lives and in our relationships with one another. Help us to grow and serve you always. Amen.

June 27

Bible Verse of the Week

One of the best ways to grow personally, and as a family, is to memorize Scripture.

This week, we have learned how Mary and Joseph were chosen to be the parents of Jesus.

Take the time to memorize Luke 1:37 with your family! Write it out and post it to your refrigerator. Let each member of your family have the opportunity to say it aloud, and then say it all together. Have fun enjoying the Word of God as a family!

Dear God, thank You for the Bible. Help us to memorize Your Word and to hide it in our hearts. Amen.

"For nothing will be impossible with God" (Luke 1:37; NASB).

Do it!

God will call each of us to do many things throughout our lifetimes. Some of these things may be life changing similar to God's call on Joseph's life, to adopt or to be obedient when things require total faith in His instructions. Some may be much smaller, such as daily tasks like doing the dishes. Whether big or small, it all matters to God. Can you think of some things God has called you to do?

Everyone is called to worship God, read their Bibles, and love their neighbors. These things are always a good place to start obeying God's leading! Do you do the small things often?

Decide to do one, small task today that honors God. By doing that small task, you are saying "yes" to God just as Mary and Joseph did!

Dear God, help us to worship You and say "yes" to you in the big and small things. We love You. Amen.

Talk About It

When we hear the stories in God's Word, we get an opportunity to learn from them. Can you imagine if you were Mary or Joseph? What would it be like to be visited by Gabriel with such an important message?

Aren't you glad that Mary and Joseph believed God and followed through with His plans? What would life be like if they hadn't?

Talk through the story of Mary and Joseph's important assignment. What details stood out to you? What do you have questions about? Discussing Bible stories are great opportunities to grow in God.

Dear God, help us to ask questions and think thoroughly about Your Word. Show us what You would like us to know about You. Amen.

June 30

Serve One Another

Can you imagine how it felt for Joseph when he found out Mary was going to have a baby before they were married? It must have been a very upsetting and confusing revelation. But an angel of God confirmed to him that Mary would be the mother of God's own Son, Jesus. Joseph was then able trust the process through which God would lead them.

Has a friend ever made a decision that was difficult for you to understand? Have you ever walked with them through a confusing situation?

When this happens in our relationships with friends and family, the best thing we can do is pray. God can handle our questions and thoughts, and He loves when we pray blessings and protection for others. Take this time to pray for someone! You never know what God has assigned to them, and your friendship can be a blessing to them.

Dear God, help us to bless one another in prayer. Please remind us to care for and uphold one another. Amen.

Eat Together

If the angel Gabriel came to visit you, would he bring angel food cake? Likely not, but you can still bake some today! Angel food cake from a boxed mix is easy to make, and it won't take too long to prepare.

Grab a box of angel food cake from the store or buy some that's already made in your store's bakery section, if you're short on time. Before serving, place some strawberries on top or drizzle chocolate sauce over each piece. Now, cut a fair share for everyone in your family to enjoy.

As you devour your cake, discuss with your family what you learned this week from the story of Mary and Joseph. What lesson can be learned by the fact that each of them said "Yes" to God's big plan for Jesus' birth? How can you say "yes" to God today?

Dear God, thank You for Your big plan to send Jesus to us! You are good, and we are grateful. Amen.

God With Us
Matthew 1:25; Luke 2:1-20

When Mary was very pregnant, Caesar Augustus called for a census to take place (all adult Hebrew men were to be counted). Each Hebrew man had to report to the town of his birth in order to be counted. Because Mary joined him in traveling to do so, Joseph walked alongside her on the long trek to his hometown of Bethlehem.

While they were in Bethlehem, the time came for Jesus to be born. They looked for a place to stay, but the only space Joseph could use was a cave where animals were kept. It was in this humble structure that Jesus, God's Son, was born.

Nearby in a field, shepherds saw an amazing spectacle of light as an angel told them of Jesus' birth. In the sky above the place of Jesus' birth, a host of God's angels proclaimed "Glory to God! Peace on Earth!" The shepherds went in search of the baby Jesus, and found Him exactly as the angel had said: He was wrapped in cloth, and lying in a feeding box. Mary and Joseph named the baby Jesus, as Mary had been told by Gabriel. Jesus was the long-prophesied Immanuel, meaning "God With Us."

Dear God, thank You for the birth of Jesus! You are faithful, and You have provided a savior for us. Amen.

July 3

A Simple Prayer

This month, we are learning about the kindness of God.

As Mary and Joseph stayed safely in Bethlehem, they experienced the kindness of God by having a place for Jesus to be born. Even though it may have been different than they might have expected, they were grateful for God's provision. We can learn from this that God is always kind to us, and He provides us everything we need when we follow Him.

During July, pray this simple prayer with your family, thanking God for His kindness over you!

Jesus, You are so kind! Thank You for giving us the kindness that leads to repentance, for loving us in our weaknesses, and for showing us grace. Teach us how to cultivate kindness in our lives and in our relationships with one another. Help us to grow and serve you always. Amen.

July 4

Bible Verse of the Week

One of the best ways to grow personally and as a family is to memorize Scripture.

This week, we learned the circumstances surrounding Jesus' birth. In His kindness God provided all Mary and Joseph needed, before and after Jesus was born.

Take the time to memorize Matthew 1:23 with your family! Write it out and post it to your refrigerator. Let each member of your family have the opportunity to say it aloud, and then say it all together. Have fun enjoying the Word of God as a family!

Dear God, thank You for the Bible. Help us to memorize Your Word and to hide it in our hearts. Amen.

"She will have a son, and they will name him Immanuel which means 'God is with us'" (Matthew 1:23, NCV).

July 5

Do it!

When the shepherds were out in the field, an angel came to tell them that Jesus had been born. It was likely an amazing sight! The Bible says there was a burst of light in the sky.

Take the opportunity tonight to look up into the sky and watch the stars, enjoy some fireworks, or use some sparklers. Use this evening to celebrate what it must have been like when the shepherds saw the burst of light and the sky filled with angels. How do you think they reacted when they received the news that the Messiah had been born?

Thank Jesus for all He has done by coming to Earth in the form of a baby!

Dear God, You are so kind to us. Thank You for sending Your Son to be with us and save us from our sins. Amen.

July 6
Talk About It

Mary and Joseph must have had a lot of questions as they prepared to be Jesus' earthly parents. Faith and trust were necessary for them to be able to do as God required of them.

Our journeys through life also require faith and trust in God. We can't see where our paths lead; only God knows what our futures hold. It's good that we have Scripture to help guide us as we pray and talk to God about where He wants us to go or what He wants us to do.

Because of His kindness toward us, God often uses His Word to remind us that He is with us. In what other ways has God shown Himself to you? The shepherds in our story were led by a light in the sky and the words of angels; in what ways has God led you?

Talk with your family today about some of the ways that God speaks to you. In what ways have you felt His comforting kindness or heard His voice?

Dear God, thank You for Your kindness in leading us with Your Word. Help us to keep our eyes and ears open to hearing Your voice. Amen.

July 7

Serve One Another

Jesus is Immanuel, the name the prophet Isaiah used when speaking of God's Son. It means "God With Us." Isn't it comforting to know that God is with us at all times? People need a reminder that God is with them because life can be full of struggles, hardships, sickness, and other difficult times.

What is a random act of kindness that you can do for someone today to show others that God is with them? Stop and say a prayer right now for God to show you a kind deed that you can do for someone. Maybe you can buy the coffee for the person behind you in line at the coffee shop and let them know God loves them. Possibly you can open the door for someone and tell them God loves them. Perhaps you can mow someone's lawn or help babysit a neighbor's child and tell them of God's kindness.

Small things matter, and those small things can mean the world to someone who needs to know that God is with them.

Dear God, show us who to serve today. We pray that You lead us to those who need to know Your kindness is always with them. Amen.

Eat Together

The shepherds searched to find Jesus in this week's story. In memory of this, let's make a trail mix of yumminess for a snack today!

Gather together with your family and find whatever ingredients you want in your trail mix. You can add popcorn, chocolate chips, dried fruit, goldfish, peanuts, or marshmallows. Place all the items in a bowl and mix well.

While you dig into your snack, talk with your family about what you learned this week through the story of Jesus' birth. What do you think Mary and Joseph were thinking as they made their way to Bethlehem and found a place for Jesus to be born? What do you think the shepherds thought when the angel came and told them about Jesus' birth? There is a lot to consider with such a special story!

Enjoy your snack while celebrating the birth of Immanuel, God With Us.

Dear God, in Your kindness, You guide us and protect us and comfort us. Thank You. Help us to care for others and comfort them, too. Amen.

Wise Men Worship Jesus
Matthew 2:1-12

July 9

Wise men from the east (places far from Bethlehem), studied the stars and planets and realized something strange was happening. A star that signified the birth of a king pointed them toward Jerusalem. They first went to Herod, to ask the new king's location. These foreign men wanted to honor and worship a king whose coming affected even the stars above. King Herod feared he would lose his position due to the power of such a king. Acting as though he also wanted to meet the new king, Herod asked his chief priests and scribes where the king would be found. They replied that Jesus would be born in Bethlehem. The wise men went to Bethlehem and located Jesus. They brought him gifts of frankincense, gold, and myrrh—gifts only given to royalty. Before they left Jesus, they had a dream that warned them about King Herod's plan to kill Jesus. They decided to avoid the evil king and take a different route back home.

Dear God, thank You for protecting Jesus and the wise men! Thank You for kindly going ahead of us and preparing the way. Amen.

A Simple Prayer

This month, we are learning about the kindness of God.

When the wise men saw the strange new star in the sky, they wanted to find Jesus in order to worship Him. At the same time, King Herod wanted to find Jesus because he was threatened by Him. Because the wise men were warned of betrayal in a dream, they returned home by an alternate route. Jesus was protected and safe. This teaches that God is kind and will often lead us to avoid difficulty if we are careful and listen to His instructions well.

During July, pray this simple prayer with your family, thanking God for His kindness over you!

Jesus, You are so kind! Thank You for giving us the kindness that leads to repentance, for loving us in our weaknesses, and for showing us grace. Teach us how to cultivate kindness in our lives and in our relationships with one another. Help us to grow and serve you always. Amen.

Bible Verse of the Week

"Where is the newborn King of the Jews? We saw his star as it rose, and we have come to worship him" (Matthew 2:2; NLT).

Persia

One of the best ways to grow personally and as a family is to memorize Scripture.

This week, we learned how the wise men honored and worshipped Jesus. God led them to His Son, just as He will lead us to find Jesus when we seek Him.

Take the time to memorize Matthew 2:2 with your family! Write it out and post it to your refrigerator. Let each person in your family have the opportunity to say it aloud, and then say it all together. Have fun enjoying the Word of God as a family!

Dear God, thank You for the Bible. Help us to memorize Your Word and to hide it in our hearts. Amen.

Do it!

God wants us to worship Him, just as the wise men did. We worship God to honor all that He did for us by becoming a baby, living on Earth, dying for our sins, and then coming back to life!

You can worship God in big ways or small ways. If you like to draw, you can draw a picture for Jesus. If you like to bake, you can bake Him a cake or cookies. If you like to dance or play sports, you can do either of those for the glory of God. Whatever you like to do, honor God today with your movement and with your time. He will love being with You, and it will bring joy to your day.

Dear God, You are worthy to be worshiped! Remind us to honor and worship You by dedicating our every moment to You. Amen.

Talk About It

This week is all about worshiping Jesus and celebrating His birth! Even though it is July, you can participate in honoring Him any time of the year. What do you do to honor God? Do you go to church to learn about Him? Do you pray and read your Bible? Do you have Bible studies with friends or spend time in a community of Christians?

Talk about a few of the ways you intentionally celebrate God as a family and with friends. Open your calendar and set aside a few dates to purposefully worship God. He would love to have a special time marked on your calendar just for Him!

Dear God, we love spending time with You. Help us to make it a priority and to put You first. Amen.

July 14

Serve One Another

This week has been centered around worshiping God and celebrating His birth. We have talked about ways to set aside time to worship Him. Can you think of a few ways that you can now worship Him by sharing His love in practical ways?

When we receive from God, it is wonderful to then give of what we've received to bless someone else! If the weather is hot where you live, you may want to bring a refreshing drink to someone who may be thirsty. Maybe you can give a neighbor kid a cool treat. Maybe you could bake some cookies to share with your family or find extra time to tidy up around the house. Whatever you do, do it with the joy and kindness of Jesus, knowing that He is worth celebrating and worth sharing.

Dear God, help us to give the love we receive from You in tangible ways to those around us. Remind us that small things matter. Amen.

Eat Together

Let's have a birthday party for Jesus! Spend the day gathering a few of your favorite snacks, beverages, and treats. Enjoy your celebration on a blanket in your backyard, or sit at a picnic table in the sunshine.

Take the opportunity to enjoy the day with your family while celebrating Jesus' birth. He was not born in fancy circumstances; He began life in a stable where the animals were kept. Swaddled in strips of cloth, this humble baby began shining His light into a dark world. The wise brought Him gifts to honor Him; you may also bring your simple meal to Jesus to honor and thank Him for what He's done. Offer up a prayer of thanks before you eat. We can celebrate Jesus' birth any time of year!

Dear God, thank You for coming into this dark world to save us! You are the best, and we worship You today. Amen.

July 16

Jesus in His Father's House
Luke 2:41-50

When Jesus was a twelve-year-old boy, He went with his parents to the Passover Feast in Jerusalem. They celebrated the Israelites' deliverance from Egypt, ate good food, and spent time with family friends. At the end of the feast, they prepared to walk home.

Mary and Joseph were on their way and assumed Jesus was with the group with whom they traveled. They walked for some time before realizing Jesus was nowhere to be found. No one had seen Him! Mary and Joseph hurried back to Jerusalem to find Him. They got more and more worried as they spent three days looking for Jesus. They finally found Him in the temple, sitting with the teachers. Jesus was asking them questions and participating in their conversations.

When Mary and Joseph asked Jesus why He had caused them such fear, He replied: "Didn't you know that I would be in My Father's House?" The three of them then traveled back to Nazareth together and Jesus continued to grow in faith and wisdom.

Dear God, help us to learn from You and listen to Your voice. Be with us as we grow in faith and wisdom. Amen.

July 17

A Simple Prayer

This month, we are learning about the kindness of God.

Even when Jesus separated Himself from Mary and Joseph and stayed behind in Jerusalem, He did not do so to be unkind. It was His kindness that prompted Him to interact with the leaders in the temple. From the beginning, Jesus was smart, wise, and showed kindness in His correction when His mother questioned Him. We can learn to be kind by following His example.

During July, pray this simple prayer with your family, thanking God for His kindness over you!

Jesus, You are so kind! Thank You for giving us the kindness that leads to repentance, for loving us in our weaknesses, and for showing us grace. Teach us how to cultivate kindness in our lives and in our relationships with one another. Help us to grow and serve you always. Amen.

Bible Verse of the Week

One of the best ways to grow personally and as a family is to memorize Scripture.

This week, we learned how Jesus sat in the Father's House with the teachers, participating in their conversations. There is no doubt His interactions with them were as kind as they were wise.

Take the time to memorize Luke 2:49 with your family! Write it out and post it to your refrigerator. Let each person in your family have the opportunity to say it aloud, and then say it all together. Have fun enjoying the Word of God as a family!

Dear God, Thank You for the Bible. Help us to memorize Your Word and to hide it in our hearts. Amen.

"Why were you searching for me?" he asked. "Didn't you know I had to be in my Father's House?" (Luke 2:49; NIV).

July 19

Do it!

Going to church is a great way to learn about and connect with God. Pastors, church leaders, and teachers can help guide Christians in their journey with Jesus. The best way to learn about and connect with God is to spend time with Him in His Word. It is also wonderful to write about Him and to Him in a journal. You can even doodle to him if you like!

Try this now by taking fifteen minutes to sit, pray, and read the Scriptures. Try to stay focused on those three things and ask God to speak to you. What do you want to tell Him? Is there anything good to thank Him for or any difficulties for which to ask His help? Is there anything in your heart you need to share with Him? He loves to listen!

When you've spent time with Him, write down a few sentences in your journal to remember what you talked about and anything you think God communicated with you. It's always nice to go back to your journal later to remind yourself of all the ways God's kindness has impacted your life!

Dear God, thank You for wanting to spend time with us! You are a loving Father who enjoys hearing from His children; help us to never forget your kindness and faithfulness to us. Amen.

Talk About It

This week, we learned about Jesus' spending time in the temple asking questions and talking with the leaders and teachers. His parents were very worried when they could not find Him, but Jesus said He was in His Father's house.

Have your parents ever gone looking for you, perhaps feeling frightened, only to end up finding you doing something good or right? Take the time to talk about this story together with your family. Share your personal stories of being found doing the right thing instead of doing the wrong thing.

Also, take a few minutes to also share a few times when you were found doing the wrong thing. How did it make you feel? What consequences did you face?

We can learn by both doing the right thing and by facing the consequences of doing the wrong thing, but it is always an easier process to be found doing something good. Spend time today sharing the differences in these processes and decide to make some good choices today.

Dear God, thank You for Your wisdom that leads us to do the right thing. Thank You for Your grace, truth, and forgiveness even when we have done the wrong thing. Amen.

July 21

Serve One Another

Jesus was found in the temple having conversations about His Father. He was likely sharing some of His insights while hearing the thoughts of the teachers and leaders. Learning is often a process of sharing our own thoughts and listening to those of others. When we take the time to share what we are learning about God with one another, we can serve each other.

Share with your family what you are currently learning about one Bible verse, life lesson, or school subject. Allow your family to ask you questions and share what they may think about the topic. Each family member should share a topic of their own and invite conversation within the family. Take the opportunity to learn from one another and teach one another something new this week. You will walk away smarter and stronger!

Dear God, thank You for all the ways we can learn from You. Help us to share with one another often, so we can know You better. Amen.

July 22

Eat Together

Time to eat together! Sharing time together in conversation will help you learn more about each other and the world you inhabit.

This week, we learned about Jesus sharing with the teachers in the temple; each added a layer of insight and knowledge. Good conversations always have layers, and so do mini pizzas. Today, you and your family will create mini pizzas with whatever toppings you like, while chatting about this week's lesson with your family. Add a topping to your pizza every time someone participates in the conversation with something helpful.

> To start off:
>
> You'll need: frozen Texas toast, shredded cheese, pepperoni, mushrooms, green peppers, and olives, or whatever toppings you prefer. Heat your Texas toast in the oven according to package directions. One at a time, as the conversation progresses, add your choice of toppings. When all pizzas are completed, place the toast back in the oven at 350 degrees for about ten minutes. Keep an eye on the toast as it bakes. Take it out of the oven when the cheese has melted. Enjoy!

Dear God, You are the best teacher of all. Help us to listen to Your words and to ask good questions. Amen.

Jesus is Baptized
Luke 1, Matthew 3, John 1

July 23

Elizabeth, Mary's cousin, was far too old to give birth to a child. An angel appeared to her to tell her she would have a boy who would prepare the people for the Messiah, Immanuel. While Elizabeth was pregnant, Mary visited her. The moment the child Elizabeth carried heard Mary's voice, he jumped for joy. He knew before he was born that Jesus was about to enter the world.

As an adult, John was very bold in speech. He lived in the wilderness near a river and often wore clothes made of camel hair. He ate honey and locusts, and he told everyone to prepare for Jesus. Even though he looked different, people listened to his messages about repentance and forgiveness. He started baptizing people with water for repentance and proclaiming that Jesus would come and baptize them in the Holy Spirit.

One day as he was preaching, Jesus also came to be baptized by John. John was overcome and felt completely unworthy, but Jesus told him, "This is the way it should be done." John obeyed and baptized Jesus. Immediately, a voice from heaven sounded "This is My Son, and I am so pleased with Him."

Dear God, help us to prepare our hearts for You. Help us to repent and ask for forgiveness where needed. Amen.

A Simple Prayer

This month, we are learning about the kindness of God.

John the Baptist called many people to repent of their sins and be baptized. God's forgiveness is available to any who will turn from their sin and purpose to live God's way.

Romans 2:4 tells us that the kindness of God leads to repentance. Let's thank God for His kindness today!

During July, pray this simple prayer with your family, thanking God for His kindness over you!

Jesus, You are so kind! Thank You for giving us the kindness that leads to repentance, for loving us in our weaknesses, and for showing us grace. Teach us how to cultivate kindness in our lives and in our relationships with one another. Help us to grow and serve you always. Amen.

July 25

Bible Verse of the Week

One of the best ways to grow personally and as a family is to memorize Scripture.

This week, we learned about John the Baptist and his ministry to the people, preparing the way for Jesus. We should also point people to Jesus, the Son of God who came to save the world.

Take the time to memorize John 1:29 with your family! Write it out and post it to your refrigerator. Let each person in your family have the opportunity to say it aloud, and then say it all together. Have fun enjoying the Word of God as a family!

Dear God, thank You for the Bible. Help us to memorize Your Word and to hide it in our hearts. Amen.

"The next day John saw Jesus coming toward him and said, "Look, the Lamb of God, who takes away the sin of the world!" (John 1:29; NIV).

July 26
Do it!

John the Baptist was really good at telling people about Jesus. He made it clear that he baptized with water, but Jesus would come to baptize people with the Holy Spirit. John knew who Jesus was and made it clear that He should be the focus. John even told that he was unworthy to untie the sandals of Jesus. By teaching the people to repent and ask for forgiveness, John helped people know who Jesus was.

How do you tell people about Jesus? Do you write songs or bring friends to church? Do you like to tell stories about what Jesus did or show Jesus' love by being kind to your neighbors?

Share about Jesus today in whatever way you choose. Tell people about His love and serve them so they can experience love in action.

Dear God, help us to teach others about You in a way that is kind. Be with us as we share Your Good News. Amen.

Talk About It

Most people learn about Jesus because someone shared His story with them. How did you come to know Him? How are you actively learning about Him?

Spend time today sharing your testimonies as a family. Tell each other how you came to know Jesus and ask one another questions. It is fun to hear each other's stories and to learn how people we care for learned about Jesus. We should be grateful that God sends us parents, friends, neighbors and a world full of people with whom we can share the gospel.

Listen carefully to one another and thank God for the people in your life who love God. Be the kind of person who shares God's love with others, too.

Dear God, thank You for sending someone to share the gospel with me. Bless those who willingly share You with others. Amen.

Serve One Another

Being baptized is such a wonderful part of the Christian life. Have you ever seen someone you know get baptized at church or in a lake or pond? Pastors and leaders in our churches can be very helpful when someone decides it's time to take the step of baptism. They can help us learn how this step of faith can bring us exciting new life.

John the Baptist baptized Jesus while many people watched; you will witness many friends and family be baptized by one another also. Spend time today asking your parents or leader at church about baptism. This is one of the practical ways we can serve Jesus and share our testimony. Leaders in your life can help you understand what the Bible says about baptism. They will love helping you take practical steps to follow the Lord in this way.

Dear God, thank You for giving us the example of John and Jesus. Help us to learn about baptism and know how to take the steps to follow You. Amen.

July 29

Eat Together

John the Baptist had a very interesting diet! You likely won't find many people eating locusts, but you will find honey in quite a few recipes. If you don't have local honey already, see if you can find a person who sells it in your town.

Take the honey you found and try it with a variety of things. You can drizzle it over apple slices or put some in hot tea. You can make a peanut butter and honey sandwich or even put it in a cookie recipe. In whatever way you want to try honey today, enjoy it while you think about the life of John the Baptist. Share with your family what you learned this week and celebrate that God's kindness leads us to repentance. Thank You, Jesus!

Dear God, You are loving, kind, and faithful. Help us to hear You, obey You, and walk with You in all we do. Amen.

Jesus Stands Up to Evil
Mark 1:12-13, Mark 4:1-11; Luke 4: 1-13

After the baptism of Jesus by John, the Holy Spirit led Jesus into the desert. For forty days He ate nothing and was tested by Satan the entire time. He kept trying to get Jesus to doubt His Father.

At first, Satan tempted Jesus to turn the stones into bread, knowing Jesus was very hungry. Jesus refused and answered Him by quoting Scripture. Then the devil took Jesus to the top of the temple and mocked Him by saying, "If you are really the Son of God, you could jump off this building and not get hurt." Jesus again answered him by quoting the Word of God. Then the devil told Jesus that he would give him all the kingdoms and riches in the world if Jesus would worship him. Still, Jesus refused while quoting Scripture. He then told Satan to go away! Angels came to help Jesus after His temptation ended.

Dear God, You are the only One worthy to be praised! Help us in our times of testing. Amen.

July 31

A Simple Prayer

This month, we are learning about the kindness of God. Even when Jesus was tempted in the desert, God showed kindness by sending angels to strengthen Him once the devil left. Even when we go through times of testing, God's kindness always remains with us. He never leaves us.

During July, pray this simple prayer with your family, thanking God for His kindness over you!

Father, You are so kind! Thank You for giving us the kindness that leads to repentance, for loving us in our weaknesses, and for showing us grace. Teach us how to cultivate kindness in our lives and in our relationships with one another. Help us to grow and serve you always. Amen.

Bible Verse of the Week

One of the best ways to grow personally and as a family is to memorize Scripture.

This week, we learned that Jesus used Scripture to fight against the temptation of Satan. The Word of God holds power!

Take the time to memorize Matthew 4:10 with your family! Write it out and post it to your refrigerator. Let each person in your family have the opportunity to say it aloud, and then say it all together. Have fun enjoying the Word of God as a family!

Dear God, thank You for the Bible. Help us to memorize Your Word and to hide it in our hearts. Amen.

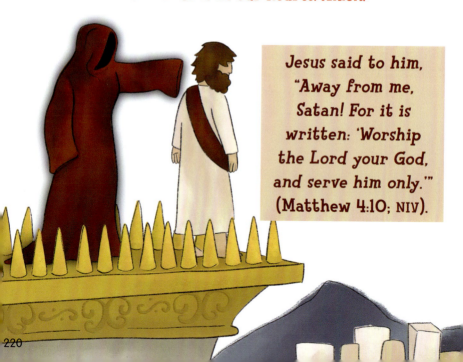

Jesus said to him, "Away from me, Satan! For it is written: 'Worship the Lord your God, and serve him only.'" (Matthew 4:10; NIV).

August 2

Do it!

In our review of Scripture this week, Jesus proved to us that Scripture is powerful! Even He used it to fight against the devil when He was being tempted in the wilderness. Speaking Scripture while trusting in His truth, is one of our best weapons against temptation and sin.

To help you remember this truth, grab a piece of paper and some markers. Draw a shield and write one of your favorite scriptures on it. Hang it up in your room or on the refrigerator. Come back to it throughout the week, or anytime you need to be encouraged!

Whenever you go through a rough time, remember that Jesus was also put into a very difficult situation when the Holy Spirit led Him into the wilderness. In the testing, He was protected and provided for by Scripture and then by angels. The Word of God will come through for you, too!

Dear God, help me to hide Your Word in my heart and to speak it out when I struggle. Be with me in difficult times and help me stay strong in You. Amen.

Talk About It

The devil tempted Jesus in the wilderness; he will also tempt us!

Have you had a circumstance in which you were trying hard to make the right decision, but struggled to do the right thing? What if there were cookies on the counter and your mom said not to have any; yet you really, really want to have one? What should you do? What if a friend wanted you to sneak out of the house and go somewhere your parents would not approve? What should you do?

The devil tried to convince Jesus to eat when He was supposed to be fasting, put Himself in danger, just to prove a point, and worship him when only God should be worshiped. None of it worked because Jesus knew who to trust. He spoke God's Word to the devil and did not fall to the temptations! The devil gave up and angels came to help Jesus.

Think about how you can prepare for the devil's tactics. All of us will be tempted. What can we do to be ready to fight against his schemes? Share ideas with your family about what each of you can do when you are tempted in some way.

Dear God, thank You for helping us prepare to make good choices. Help us to stand strong when we're tempted and always rely on You. Amen.

August 4

Serve One Another

The devil can be tricky when he wants to tempt you to do something wrong. Even though he can be tricky, he doesn't have to win your attention! Jesus is always stronger, and you can fight off the attacks of the enemy by being prepared ahead of time.

Do you have an accountability partner or a friend who helps you when you struggle with something? Accountability partners are a great idea because they can encourage you when the devil tries to tempt you. If you are struggling in a certain area, you can tell your friend about it. When that sin or temptation comes lurking around the corner, you can fight back with Scripture! If you are having a hard time, your accountability partner can pray for you!

By having friends and family members who help us fight when we're tempted, we can stay strong and withstand temptation. This is an excellent way to serve one another.

Dear God, thank You for the people in my life who help me stay encouraged in You. Please give me good friends who ask me good questions and who love me well. Amen.

Eat Together

Jesus must have been very hungry when He was in the wilderness. But when the devil tried to tempt Him to eat bread, Jesus refused. What a perfect Savior He is!

Thankfully, we can eat bread that the Lord provides for us, and we can have our bellies filled. What is your favorite type of bread? Do you prefer whole wheat, white, rye, sourdough, or pumpernickel? If you are up to it, bake your favorite type of bread to add to your dinner this evening. If not, pick some up from the store.

While you eat tonight, thank God for His perfection in the wilderness. Encourage your family members to stay filled with God's Word so they can fight off the tactics of the devil.

Dear God, thank You for bread to eat. Help us to be filled with Your Word so we can operate with gratitude and strength. Amen.

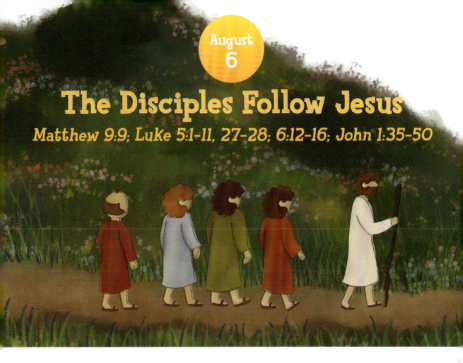

August 6

The Disciples Follow Jesus
Matthew 9:9; Luke 5:1-11, 27-28; 6:12-16; John 1:35-50

After His temptation in the wilderness, Jesus went on to teach people at the Sea of Galilee. Large crowds of people came to listen to Him speak. He began to choose those who would be closest to Him. He didn't pick those who were rich or educated or considered special. Instead, He chose young men who fished for their food, a tax collector, and even a traitor!

As time went on, Jesus taught these twelve young men what it looked like to listen to God, to pray, and to help people. As most of them knew how to fish for food, He also showed them how to fish for people with His love. He did many miracles among them, and they were amazed.

Dear God, Thank You for choosing us to know You. Help us to say "yes" when You ask us to follow. Amen.

A Simple Prayer

This month, we are learning how God gives us new life. Even when we have made mistakes in the past and will again in the future, God brings us salvation through His Son! We can receive new life through Jesus when we repent and accept Him as Lord and Savior of our lives.

During August, pray this simple prayer with your family, thanking God for the new life He offers you!

Jesus, thank you for new life and fresh starts. You make us new in You. Teach us how to cultivate the fruit of new life in our days and in our relationships with one another. Help us to grow and serve you always. Amen.

August 8

Bible Verse of the Week

One of the best ways to grow personally and as a family is to memorize Scripture.

This week, we learned about how young men who were not educated or wealthy chose to follow Jesus. It's amazing that this group of men literally changed the world!

Take the time to memorize Matthew 4:19 with your family! Write it out and post it to your refrigerator. Let each person in your family have the opportunity to say it aloud, and then say it all together. Have fun enjoying the Word of God as a family!

Dear God, thank You for the Bible. Help us to memorize Your Word and to hide it in our hearts. Amen.

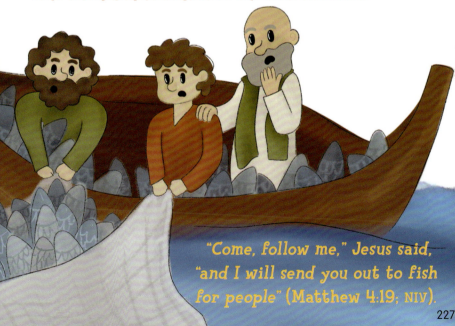

"Come, follow me," Jesus said, "and I will send you out to fish for people" (Matthew 4:19, NIV).

August 9

Do it!

Time to get a little creative! Grab some paper and draw a bunch of fish. Cut the fish out and set them aside. Get a pencil and some dental floss or other type of string. Tape the dental floss to the end of the pencil like a fishing pole. Borrow a bowl from the kitchen and put the handmade fish inside. Then lean the "fishing pole" against the bowl with the string dangling inside like a fishing line. Set this decoration somewhere you will see it often this week.

Whenever you see your little craft, remember how Jesus was a fisher of men! Throughout His time with His disciples, He often used fish and fishing as a way to tell stories about His Father. You can read these stories and learn about your Father in heaven, too.

Dear Jesus, you are a fisher of men! Help me to learn about Father God this week through Your journey with the disciples. Amen.

Talk About It

This week's lesson is filled with stories about fish! The disciples were very familiar with fishing for food because several of them were fishermen by trade. By telling stories about fishing, Jesus was helping His disciples learn about God in a way they could understand. Jesus told His disciples that even though they were used to fishing for food, He would teach them how to fish for people. What do you think it means to fish for people?

Jesus shared the story of His Father to teach the disciples, the disciples would one day tell the story of Jesus to people! They would encourage people to believe in Him, repent, and be saved.

How can you fish for people in your life? Talk with your family this week about how it looks to share the gospel with others. What are your favorite ways to tell people about Jesus?

Dear Jesus, thank You for fishing for me! Help me to become a successful fisher of men for You. Amen.

August 11

Serve One Another

This week, try sharing the love of Jesus with others! You may choose to share a favorite Bible verse with a friend, or offer to pray for someone who needs it. You may decide to volunteer at church or in your neighborhood to help out. You can find many ways to send a little love into your community and be a fisher of men.

When we follow Jesus, we should live a life of service wherever we go. Small acts of kindness like opening the door for a stranger or smiling at someone who looks sad can be a small but mighty way to love those around you! When Jesus asks you today to follow Him, you can do so by loving those He brings into your path.

Dear God, send me a small assignment as I follow You today! Help me to say "yes" to You and help others learn of You. Amen.

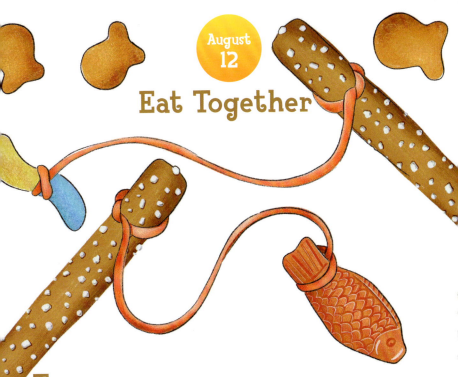

August 12

Eat Together

Today is a good day for a little sweet treat! Go to the store and find several snacks that are fish related, like goldfish crackers, or Swedish fish, or maybe even something with sharks or jellyfish involved! Join with your family in a grocery story scavenger hunt to locate fish themed snacks. Purchase your favorites and take them home.

While at home snacking, talk about what it was like to fish for your food today. Even the disciples looked for their food before they could take it home to eat. Though "fishing" at the grocery store is a little different than fishing in water, it gives you an idea of what it's like to search for treasures from God.

Dear God, help us to love and laugh while we fish for food and for people. Remind us of Your goodness with everything we do. Amen.

One Man Thanks Jesus

Luke 17: 11-19

Jesus was on His way to Jerusalem when he saw ten lepers who were standing away from the crowd. Because of their contagious skin disease, they were not allowed to be near other people. They had to live far away from the cities and had little food. These particular lepers heard that Jesus could help them, and they cried out to Him.

Jesus told them to go show themselves to the priests to prove their healing, even though they still had leprosy. As the men headed toward the priests, they were healed of their skin diseases! One man who was healed ran back to Jesus to thank Him for such a gift. Because this man was the only one of the ten lepers to return and give glory to Jesus, He replied: "You were the only one to give glory to God. Now go, your faith has healed you."

Dear God, thank You for Your healing power. Help us to always remember to thank You when You heal us. Amen.

August 14

A Simple Prayer

This month, we are learning about how God gives us new life.

When the lepers cried out to Jesus, He healed them. Only one of the men came back to thank Him, and Jesus gave that man a new life. The one leper was thankful and gave all glory to Jesus!

During August, pray this simple prayer with your family, thanking God for the new life He's given you!

Jesus, thank you for new life and fresh starts. You make us new in You. Teach us how to cultivate the fruit of new life in our days and in our relationships with one another. Help us to grow and serve you always. Amen.

Bible Verse of the Week

One of the best ways to grow personally and as a family is to memorize Scripture.

This week, we learned the story of how Jesus healed ten lepers. One was grateful and returned to give Jesus thanks and praise.

Take the time to memorize Luke 17:16 with your family! Write it out and post it to your refrigerator. Let each person in your family have the opportunity to say it aloud, and then say it all together. Have fun enjoying the Word of God as a family!

Dear God, thank You for the Bible. Help us to memorize Your Word and to hide it in our hearts. Amen.

"He threw himself at Jesus' feet and thanked him" (Luke 17:16; NIRV).

August 16
Do it!

Gratitude is one of the best ways we can celebrate the new life Jesus gives us. People often think of gratitude at Thanksgiving, but we can practice thankfulness at any time of the year. In fact, being grateful every day is one of the best ways to live fully.

In what ways has God healed or helped you? When have you seen Him come through for you? Take time today to make a gratitude list of at least ten ways that Jesus has given you a blessed new life! Celebrate all that Jesus has done and then tell someone else about it. By giving the glory back to Jesus, we show the world how faith looks.

Dear God, help us to be faithful. Thank You for the new life only You can provide. Amen.

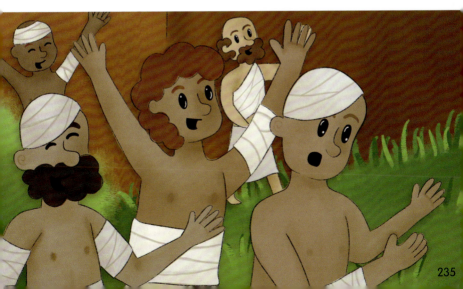

Talk About It

Jesus wants us to be thankful in everyday life and in every circumstance. That can seem tough, can't it? It's easy to want to complain when things aren't going our way, and it's easy to forget to thank God when He heals us or helps us.

What are a few practical ways to remain thankful everyday? How can you encourage yourself and others in your family to be grateful for all the things that come into your lives?

By encouraging one another and reminding each other to give thanks, honor, and glory to God, we live out our faith in the way God desires. Abundant blessing is found in a grateful life!

Dear God, please show us how to exude gratitude every day. We want to worship and honor You fully. Amen.

August 18

Serve One Another

Have you ever done something good for someone without taking any credit? It's a wonderful thing to do! Sometimes it's easy to do something good for someone else because we want to receive an award or receive praise. That is exactly the opposite of what Jesus says to do! He says in Matthew 6:3 that when you show acts of kindness, don't let the left hand know what the right hand is doing. This means, do something good because it's the right thing to do, not because you will get rewarded. Doing good things in secret is a way to honor God.

Make a point to do something good today without telling anyone. By doing a good deed in secret, the receiver can thank God for His generosity. God will get the credit and the praise!

Dear God, Forgive us for the ways we have tried to take credit for doing good. Help us to do good in secret. Amen.

August 19

Eat Together

Thanksgiving is a day set aside to be grateful for all God has done. Turkey and all the trimmings are the traditional feast that most enjoy. This makes turkey a great reminder to be a grateful person, even when it's not actually Thanksgiving Day.

Decide along with your family a way to enjoy turkey today. It could be layered on a sandwich, stacked on a charcuterie board, turkey burgers on the grill, or turkey sausage with eggs and toast.

Partaking of food that reminds us of gratitude can change our focus and attitude. From now on, when you eat turkey in any form, be reminded of the ways that Jesus has healed and helped you. Celebrate the new life He's given you with every bite.

While enjoying your meal, share with your family what you learned about Jesus this week. What stood out to you? What surprised you? What will you take away?

Dear God, we are thankful for You! Give us eyes to see and ears to hear the ways You have provided and the new life You have granted us. Amen.

August 20

The Sermon on the Mount
Matthew 5–7

Jesus spent a lot of His time speaking to the people, teaching them about the ways of His Father and His kingdom. While He was in Galilee, He went on a mountain to share with the group of people who followed Him. This speech would later be called The Sermon on the Mount. In this sermon, He shared important principles about life in His kingdom. He taught that those who mourn will be comforted, those who seek righteousness will find it, and the pure in heart will see God. He explained how to pray and taught how important it is to obey the law. He taught many things in this, His longest recorded sermon. The people listened, and they were amazed.

Dear God, You are an amazing Teacher! Help us to follow Your teachings and to do what is right as we learn new life in You. Amen.

August 21

A Simple Prayer

This month, we are learning about how God gives us new life.

When Jesus gave His Sermon on the Mount to the crowd, He shared about how new life in Jesus really looks. He told them that obeying the law and following the teachings of God's kingdom, would create for them a blessed new life. Jesus shared truths of the Kingdom with all who would listen.

During August, pray this simple prayer with your family, thanking God for the new life He has given you!

Jesus, thank you for new life and fresh starts. You make us new in You. Teach us how to cultivate the fruit of new life in our days and in our relationships with one another. Help us to grow and serve you always. Amen.

August 22

Bible Verse of the Week

One of the best ways to grow personally and as a family is to memorize Scripture.

This week, we learned about kingdom life as Jesus taught us about blessing. The new life He wants us to have will result in a grateful heart and a blessed life.

Take the time to memorize Matthew 6:33 with your family! Write it out and post it to your refrigerator. Let each person in your family have the opportunity to say it aloud, and then say it all together. Have fun enjoying the Word of God as a family!

Dear God, thank You for the Bible. Help us to memorize Your Word and to hide it in our hearts. Amen.

> "But seek first the Kingdom of God and His righteousness, and all these things shall be added to you" (Matthew 6:33; NKJV).

August 23

Do it!

The Sermon on the Mount is full of amazing wisdom. Jesus taught the people His ways that lead to blessing. He talked about the poor in the spirit, those who mourn, and those who are meek. He talked about those who hunger and thirst for righteousness, the merciful, and the pure in heart. He also talked about the peacemakers, and those who are persecuted for the sake of Jesus.

Open your Bible to Matthew 5. Read through The Sermon on the Mount carefully and choose one verse to focus on throughout this week. Write the verse on a notecard and paste it to your school folder or bathroom mirror—anywhere you will be sure to see it each day. Thank Jesus for His wisdom and do your best to follow it!

Dear God, help me to follow You and live my life in the ways You will bless. Shine Your light through me. Amen.

August 24

Talk About It

This week, we have been spending time in Matthew 5—7 and talking about the Sermon on the Mount. Sometimes this passage of Scripture is also referred to as the Beatitudes. Yesterday, you chose to focus on one of the verses of this sermon. Why did you choose that one? Is that Beatitude easier or more difficult for you to follow than the others?

Look through all the verses in the Sermon on the Mount and talk with your family about them. If you could list them in order of the easiest to follow all the way to the hardest, how would your list look?

Compare your list to your family members'. Talk through how you can each encourage to put them into practice in daily life.

Dear God, thank you for Your blessings. Help us to live a life that honors Your teachings. Amen.

August 25

Serve One Another

God's Kingdom is one of service. When we live our lives according to the ways Jesus calls "blessed," we can be a blessing and gift to others. When we give to, work on behalf of, or help someone else, we are honoring Jesus.

Think through the Beatitudes. Choose one that is difficult for you and memorize it. Ask God to bring a situation into your life in which you can walk out that specific truth. If His answer to your prayer brings about a difficult situation, try not to complain. Remember He is giving you an opportunity to serve Him just as you asked. Seeking God for ways that you can bring Him glory enables you to be part of the work of His kingdom on Earth!

Dear God, send me opportunities to serve You and Your Kingdom. Let me live out my calling as a child of God. Amen.

August 26

Eat Together

One of the Beatitudes from this week's lesson is: "Blessed are those who hunger and thirst for righteousness, for they shall be filled" (Matthew 5:6; NKJV). The "Eat Together" section appears throughout this devotional. You've had the opportunity to eat together often. Aren't you thankful God provides good food and snacks?

Because it's such a gift to share a meal, take this opportunity to shop for a few items at the grocery store in order to donate to a local food kitchen or food bank. You can pick up canned goods, boxed meals, and other non-perishable items. While doing so, pick up a few of the same items for your family.

When you return home, cook a meal with the boxes or cans of food you bought for your family. While eating, pray for the local people in your community who are hungry and thank God for His provision. Drop off the extra groceries sometime soon and thank God you were able to participate in His provision in this way.

Dear God, help those who are hungry, both for food and for righteousness. Show me how to contribute and be part of the solution. Amen.

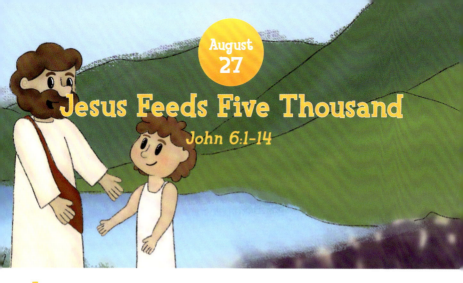

August 27

Jesus Feeds Five Thousand

John 6:1-14

Jesus went up on a mountainside with His disciples. Because He had been doing miracles and healing the sick, a large crowd of people followed Him. It was almost time to eat, and even though he already knew the answer, Jesus said to Philip, one of His disciples: "Where can we buy bread for these people to eat?" Philip responded with confusion; it would have cost an entire year's wages to feed so many people.

Another disciple told Jesus that a boy in the crowd had five loaves of bread and two fish. They all knew the boy's small lunch wouldn't come close to feeding all the people who were there. But Jesus had the people sit down. He took the bread and fish and thanked God for them; then He instructed the disciples to hand out the food until every person had their fill. People ate until they were satisfied. Jesus then told the disciples to collect the leftovers, so nothing was wasted. The disciples collected twelve baskets of extra food!

Dear God, thank You for doing miracles like feeding five thousand people with five loaves of bread and two fish. You are amazing! Amen.

August 28

A Simple Prayer

This month, we are learning about how God gives us new life.

When Jesus miraculously fed the five thousand, He showed us He is always able to care for us, no matter the circumstance. He shared about how new life in Him really looks like by feeding all the people until they were full. By being grateful for our provision and by trusting in God's faithfulness, we are sure to witness Jesus' work in our lives, as well.

During August, pray this simple prayer with your family, thanking God for the new life He's given you!

Jesus, thank you for new life and fresh starts. You make us new in You. Teach us how to cultivate the fruit of new life in our days and in our relationships with one another. Help us to grow and serve you always. Amen.

Bible Verse of the Week

"Then Jesus took the loaves of bread, thanked God for them, and gave them to the people who were sitting there" (John 6:11; NCV).

One of the best ways to grow personally and as a family is to memorize Scripture.

This week, we learned how Jesus multiplied food for a huge crowd. Anything given to Jesus becomes more that it was before!

Take the time to memorize John 6:11 with your family! Write it out and post it to your refrigerator. Let each person in your family have the opportunity to say it aloud, and then say it all together. Have fun enjoying the Word of God as a family!

Dear God, thank You for the Bible. Help us to memorize Your Word and to hide it in our hearts. Amen.

August 30

Do it!

One of the ways to please God is to say a blessing over the food before eating. Just as Jesus blessed the five loaves and two fish, we have the opportunity to thank God for our meals. Whether you are at breakfast, lunch, or dinner, take a moment to be grateful for the food God has provided for you. Maybe you love what's on your plate or maybe you aren't fond of it; but no matter what, meals are a gift of God to us! Blessing your food and being grateful for whatever is provided, can help you remember God's goodness, as well as those who may have less to eat than you do.

Thank God for your meals today and be blessed!

Dear God, thank You for food to eat, no matter the flavor or texture. Help us to be grateful for what we have. Please use it to nourish our bodies with the nutrients we need. Amen.

August 31
Talk About It

Y ou are most likely familiar with the word "multiply." It simply means to increase or to reproduce. Just as Jesus multiplied the loaves and the fish, He also multiplies our faith and our joy as we trust and obey Him.

Can you think of anything in your life that God has multiplied? Perhaps there was a time when you needed a friend and He gave you a few! Maybe you asked God for something small and He answered with something even bigger.

Talk with your family today about the ways you have seen God multiply good in your lives. Celebrate and thank God for being Your provider and for giving His people new life.

Dear God, thank You for multiplying good in my life. Help me to remember to be grateful for all the ways You abundantly provide. Amen.

September 1

Serve One Another

Just as Jesus served the crowd by blessing the food and multiplying it, we can also serve others by asking God to bless and multiply our efforts.

Whatever you do, you can commit your work to God in prayer. Ask Him to bless you and your work, so that you can be a blessing to those around you. Perhaps you like to help others by cleaning, doing chores, or babysitting. Maybe you are employed or help take care of a parent or grandparent. Ask God to multiply His love and service in simple and profound ways as you serve. Pray this prayer whenever you purpose to give God your efforts.

Dear God, thank You for giving me the ability to serve others. Please bless me as I do my work, bless the effort I put into it, and bless those around me who will receive it. Amen.

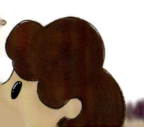

Eat Together

Snacks don't have to be complicated to multiply! Just as God multiplied the loaves and the fish, you can find many foods at the grocery store that are labeled buy one, get one (BOGO) or BOGO half off.

Take a trip to the store with your family. Look specifically for one food or drink item that is BOGO. Take it home to enjoy with your family. Sit together at the table and thank God for His gift of multiplication! Jesus has not changed; He still gives us opportunities to give thanks for receiving His gift of provision.

Dear God, thank You for all the ways You multiply our food, gifts, and time. Help us to pay attention to the little things in life that speak of Your love, no matter how simple or small. Amen.

September 3

Above the Waves
Matthew 14:22-33; Mark 6:45-52; John 6:16-21

Jesus completed the miracle of multiplying the loaves and fish, then went to a mountainside alone to pray. He had His disciples sail the boat across the Sea of Galilee so He could be with God. As he prayed, a storm hit the area, causing rain, lightning, and wind. The waves on the Sea of Galilee were huge and chaotic. He knew His friends would be frightened.

Jesus walked down the mountain, over the shore, and continued walking on the water as if it were solid! He walked close to where the boat was being tossed about by the waves. His disciples were terrified when they saw Him, thinking Jesus was a ghost. Jesus calmed their fear when He replied, "Do not be afraid! It's Me!" Peter urged Jesus to invite him to walk on the water too, and Jesus did. Peter got out of the boat and walked toward Jesus. As long as he kept his eyes on Jesus, he didn't sink. The moment Peter looked at the waves and rain, he sank beneath the churning sea. He called out to Jesus: "Help me! I'm afraid!"

Jesus caught him, and asked Peter the reason he had such little faith. As soon as Jesus and Peter entered the boat, the storm stopped. All the disciples were amazed and worshiped Jesus.

Dear God, thank You for peace in the middle of the storms of life. Help us to be brave and to keep our eyes on You. Amen.

A Simple Prayer

This month, we are learning about how God gives us patience. When Jesus caught Peter so that he did not drown, Jesus showed Peter his grace and patience. He showed us what patience is by caring for Peter even when Peter doubted His power. By keeping our eyes on Jesus, we can experience the safety and security He brings.

During September, pray this simple prayer with your family, thanking God for His patience with you!

Jesus, you are the perfect example of patience! Thank you for working in us to make us steadfast and faithful. Teach us how to cultivate patience in our lives and in our relationships with one another. Help us to grow and serve you always. Amen.

Bible Verse of the Week

"Trust in the lord with all your heart; do not depend on your own understanding" (Proverbs 3:5, NLT).

One of the best ways to grow personally and as a family is to memorize Scripture.

This week, we learned that Jesus is perfectly capable of walking on water. When we have faith in Him and His power, no storms of life can cause us to sink.

Take the time to memorize Proverbs 3:5 with your family! Write it out and post it to your refrigerator. Let each member of your family have the opportunity to say it aloud, and then say it all together. Have fun enjoying the Word of God as a family!

Dear God, thank You for the Bible. Help us to memorize Your Word and to hide it in our hearts. Amen.

September 6
Do it!

Just as Peter had to fix his eyes on Jesus in order keep from sinking, we need to keep our eyes and hearts focused on Him as well. Sometimes God calls us to trust Him, even when we can't see what's ahead of us or even when we don't know what to do. Thank goodness Jesus gives us friends and family to help us on our journey to know Him.

Have a staring contest with a friend or family member today. See which of you can look the other in the eyes the longest, without blinking or looking away. Simply by practicing eye contact, we get a glimpse of the sweetness of keeping our eyes on someone we love. Have a few laughs together as you see how long you can go without blinking!

Dear God, we can trust in You. Help us to always keep our eyes on You, never looking away. You are faithful to keep us safe in You. Amen.

September 7

Talk About It

Have you ever been caught in a big storm? You may not have been on a boat like the disciples, but perhaps you still experienced heavy rain, ferocious wind, and flashing lightning. Describe for your family how you felt while you watched the storm. Each of you can share about some storms you have witnessed, whether weather related or chaotic life circumstances that felt as though a storm had hit your life. What were some of the emotions you felt? Did you cry or pray? Did you recite Scripture aloud or sit in silence?

Storms come into our lives in a variety of ways. Just as Peter had to trust in God, so do we. The next time you are in a storm of any kind, call out to Jesus. Pray and ask for His help in your time of need. Know that He is listening and watching out for you.

Dear God, thank You for protecting us in life's storms. Help us to pray, watch, and listen for Your instruction and Your help when we are in trouble. Amen.

September 8

Serve One Another

Natural disasters and storms happen in many places throughout the world. Tornados, hurricanes, tsunamis, and many other catastrophic natural events cause damage, destruction, and turmoil.

Sit down with your family and research a few organizations that help with natural disasters or storms. Find out if you can donate money, clothing, or other items to them or directly to someone who has been affected by a storm. Even if the storm wasn't recent, it can take years to recover from massive natural disasters. By lending a helping hand or donating to someone who needs it, you can love like Jesus and lift people up who need it the most.

Thank God for His protection and provision while recovering from the storms of life and ask Him to give you patience and endurance while you overcome difficulties.

Dear God, please bless all those who have been affected by the storms of life. Help us to give to them and serve them in practical ways when hard times come. Amen.

September 9

Eat Together

Life is full of waves and sometimes even storms. We've learned about different kinds of storms this week while studying the story of Jesus walking on water. He called Peter to come to Him on the water and was patient with Him even when Peter sank because of doubt. In just the same way, Jesus will be patient with us when we struggle during the storms that hit our lives.

Today, let's share a snack together that resembles the waves that tossed Peter's boat. We can use fun or familiar things to remind us of the things we learn about our Lord. So let's look at some chips; they can be potato chips, corn chips, sweet potato chips, veggie chips, or even banana or apple chips. As you enjoy your chips, keep an eye out for one that has a wave in it. Try to find a few of them and share them with your family. Do any of them look like the type of waves that were rocking the disciples' boat?

While enjoying the curves of your favorite chip, chat with your family about what you learned this week while considering the story of Jesus walking on the water. What stood out to you and why?

Dear God, thank You for showing us how to trust You this week. Help us to be brave, to step out in faith, and to keep our eyes on You. Amen.

Who is Your Neighbor?
Luke 10:25-37

September 10

A man asked Jesus what he needed to do to go to heaven. Jesus responded with a question: "What is written in the Law?" The man answered, "Love the Lord your God with all your heart and all your soul and with all your strength and with all your mind, and love your neighbor as yourself."

Jesus replied, "Yes. Do this, and you will live."

Trying to find a way to justify himself, the man asked, "Who is my neighbor?" Jesus then told a story about an Israelite man who was robbed and left for dead on the side of the road. As the man lay suffering, a priest walked by and did not stop to help. Then, a Levite walked by and did not help either. Soon after, a Samaritan man walked by, stopped to help, and even paid for others to take care of him long after he could. We must note here that Samaritans and Israelites were traditionally enemies.

Jesus asked the man, "Which of these three do you think was a neighbor to the robbed man?" The man said the Samaritan was the good neighbor. Jesus finished, "Now go and do likewise."

Dear God, thank you for the example of the kindness and patience of the Samaritan man. Help us to slow down and show mercy to others. Amen.

A Simple Prayer

This month, we are learning about how God gives us patience.

When the Samaritan man stopped to care for the robbed man, he patiently set his own plans aside and showed mercy to the injured man. Taking the time to slow down and care for others requires us to be patient, considering our own plans of less importance than the healing and recovery of another. We can be like the Samaritan man and love our neighbors well by putting their needs first.

During September, pray this simple prayer with your family, thanking God for His patience with you!

Jesus, you are the perfect example of patience! Thank you for working in us to make us steadfast and faithful. Teach us how to cultivate patience in our lives and in our relationships with one another. Help us to grow and serve you always. Amen.

Bible Verse of the Week

> "You must love the Lord your God with all your heart, all your soul, all your mind, and all your strength. [And] Love your neighbor as yourself. No other commandment is greater than these" (Mark 12:29-31, NLT).

One of the best ways to grow personally and as a family is to memorize Scripture.

This week, we learned the story of the Good Samaritan. This kind and patient man set his own plans aside to help a stranger who had been robbed and beaten. He even paid the expenses for the injured man while he rested and healed.

Take the time to memorize Mark 12:29–31 with your family! Write it out and post it to your refrigerator. Let each person in your family have the opportunity to say it aloud, and then say it all together. Have fun enjoying the Word of God as a family!

Dear God, thank You for the Bible. Help us to memorize Your Word and to hide it in our hearts. Amen.

September 13
Do it!

Wherever you live, school is likely in session. Your teachers and coaches slow down to be patient and gracious with you while you study and learn. They are also patient and kind with kids who may be bullied like the man in our story about the Samaritan.

Though you won't likely need to pay the hospital fees for someone who has been mistreated, you can still love your teachers, coaches, fellow students, or neighbors when life has treated them badly.

Think of a neighbor or friend who could use a little love today. Take them a small gift like a box of cookies or some fresh fruit. Thank them for being part of your life and for being a good friend. Being generous to others is a wonderful way to love your neighbor.

Dear God, remind me to think of others and their needs. Help me to be kind, patient, and generous to my neighbors. Amen.

September 14

Talk About It

This week's story highlights the responses of three different men toward their robbed and injured neighbor. Both the priest and the Levite passed by the man who was hurt. Even though they were considered holy men, they didn't stop to help their neighbor. The Samaritan man, who was considered an enemy to the people in Jerusalem, was the only one who stopped. Not only did he stop, but he helped bandage the man's wounds and pay for a place for him to stay while he got better.

What are your thoughts about the three men in the story? Which one do you most relate to? Do you stop to help your hurting neighbor? Or do you often walk on by? Talk with your family about how it looks to love the people around you in a real and kind way. How does it feel when you help others? Why?

Dear God, thank you for stopping to help us when we are hurt and wounded. Help us to do the same for others around us. Amen.

Serve One Another

Many people in our world are wounded, hurt, and recovering in some way. Do you ever consider the people around you and the struggles they are going through? How does the knowledge that they are hurting impact you? When you are hurt and struggling, what do you do?

Today, join with your family and put together a first aid kit with bandages and ointments to keep in your family car. This will enable you to be prepared in case someone falls, gets injured, or needs some help. Being prepared ahead of time means you will be able to offer help right away when someone is injured. Something as simple as a bandage can mean a lot to the person who needs one!

Dear God, help me to be prepared and ready to help in times of need. Show me how to be loving by thinking of others ahead of time. Amen.

September 16

Eat Together

Whenever you are recovering from sickness or injury, comfort food can help. What are some of your favorite comfort foods? Some people like chicken soup, ginger ale, mashed potatoes, mac and cheese, or even fried chicken. Choose a comfort food of your liking and share it together as a family.

Sit at the table and talk about what you learned this week. What stood out to you most about the story of the Good Samaritan? What made you stop and think? Have you heard this story before or was it the first time?

Thank God for the wisdom of the Scriptures and pray together as a family while enjoying your comforting meal or snack.

Dear God, You are faithful to take care of us. Help us remember to care for others, whether they are our friends, family, or strangers in need. Amen.

September 17

Sibling Rivalry
Luke 10:38-42

Jesus went to visit Bethany, a small town near Jerusalem where two sisters named Mary and Martha lived with their brother, Lazarus. The sisters invited Jesus and His disciples to share a meal with them and Jesus agreed to come. Martha began to hurriedly prepare the house and food for His visit.

When Jesus arrived, Martha stayed busy serving and caring for her guests' needs. Mary, instead, sat at the feet of Jesus and enjoyed His company. She listened to Him teach and share. Martha got flustered and frustrated and asked Jesus, "Can you please tell Mary to help me? I am doing all the work while she just sits there."

Jesus looked at Martha warmly and replied, "My dear Martha, you are worried and upset about all these details. But there is only one thing you really need. And your sister, Mary, knows what that is!" Jesus responded this way because being with Jesus is always better than doing things for Him.

Dear God, thank You for the example of Mary and Martha. Help me to remember to spend time with You before trying to do things for You. Amen.

September 18

A Simple Prayer

This month, we are learning about how God gives us patience.

When Martha was upset with her sister Mary for not helping, Jesus was patient with Martha and He also patiently sat with Mary for a visit.

During September, pray this simple prayer with your family, thanking God for His patience with you!

Jesus, you are the perfect example of patience! Thank you for working in us to be steadfast and faithful. Teach us how to cultivate patience in our lives and in our relationships with one another. Help us to grow and serve you always. Amen.

September 19

Bible Verse of the Week

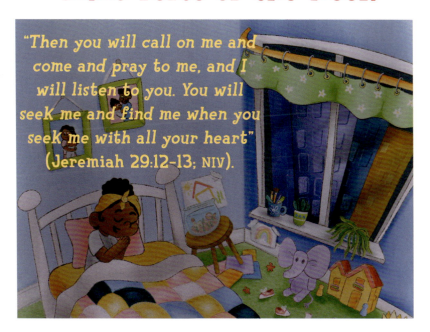

"Then you will call on me and come and pray to me, and I will listen to you. You will seek me and find me when you seek me with all your heart" (Jeremiah 29:12-13; NIV).

One of the best ways to grow personally and as a family is to memorize Scripture.

This week, we learned how Mary and Martha served Jesus in different ways. One served by taking care of practical needs, while the other served Jesus by learning the ways of His kingdom.

Take the time to memorize Jeremiah 29:12–13 with your family! Write it out and post it to your refrigerator. Let each person in your family have the opportunity to say it aloud, and then say it all together. Have fun enjoying the Word of God as a family!

Dear God, thank You for the Bible. Help us to memorize Your Word and to hide it in our hearts. Amen.

September 20
Do it!

Life can feel rushed and busy, just as it did for Martha. We can spend so much time doing things for Jesus that we can forget to spend time with Him. It's important to remember that sitting at Jesus' feet and learning from Him through prayer and by reading the Bible are our most important comissions.

Prioritize your time with God this week. Spend fifteen minutes reading the Bible and praying each morning. At bedtime, spend another fifteen minutes telling God about your day and thanking Him for the chance to serve Him!

If you struggle with praying, try to make these prayer times a new goal for you. See how prayer transforms your life when you give Jesus your heart first thing every day. He will fill your heart with His love and you can serve Him from the overflow of that love. Write your thoughts about prayer and spending time with Jesus and share them with your family.

Dear God, the most important thing I can do is spend time with You. Help me to remember to make our time together a priority. Amen.

Talk About It

Mary and Martha certainly had different personalities. Mary preferred to spend quality time with Jesus while Martha served Him by caring for His practical needs. It's important to live out both of these examples in our walk with God. We need to take time to know Jesus, as well as serve others in His name.

Do you tend to like quality time or practical serving better? Do you ever struggle with simply sitting quietly and being with Jesus? Why or why not? Likewise, do you ever struggle with serving God by serving others? Why do you think this is so?

Talk with your family about their different personality types. Encourage one another to sit still with Jesus and also in serving Him in practical ways.

Dear God, thank You for desiring quality time with me. Help me to be equally still enough to simply be with You and eager to serve You in practical ways. Amen.

September 22

Serve One Another

Mary spent quality time with Jesus by sitting at His feet, listening to Him teach. Because Jesus was right there with her; it was easy for her to give Him her full attention. Though Jesus is not physically present with us, we can give Him our full attention by praying and spending time in His Word.

If you have trouble focusing while trying to spend time with Jesus, you can add a prayer list to your routine. As you become aware of prayer needs of family and friends, list them and keep them in your Bible. While spending time with God each morning or each night, pray for the people on your list. By focusing on the needs of those around you, you are serving others while also spending time with God. You can even write notes in the margins of the paper as you see God answer your prayers.

Dear God, help me be intentional about setting aside time to spend with You every day. Make me aware of the prayer needs of my family and friends. Amen.

September 23

Eat Together

Just as Martha did, we often get so busy trying to serve visitors in our home that we forget to pay attention to our guests. It's important to have a well-cared-for house and food to serve guests; but even more important is the time spent with friends.

Talk with your family and decide on a few drinks or food items that take little time to prepare. Make sure you have these in your home in case a visitor drops by. Have coffee and tea handy all the time. This way, you know you have something quick to serve and can spend time with them instead of worrying about preparing food!

Sit down with your family today and have a hot beverage while you talk about the story of Mary and Martha. Celebrate spending time with one another and discuss how to live a less hectic and complicated life.

Dear God, thank You for time spent with friends and family. Remind me that spending simple time together is better than a perfect meal or the cleanest house. Amen.

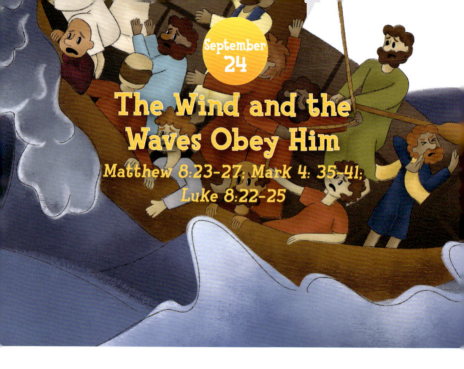

The Wind and the Waves Obey Him

September 24

Matthew 8:23-27; Mark 4: 35-41; Luke 8:22-25

After teaching and ministering to crowds of people, Jesus and His disciples boarded a boat to cross the Sea of Galilee. Jesus fell asleep and was not awakened when a horrendous storm blew up. The disciples thought they were going to sink from the massive waves and whirling wind.

The disciples shouted to Him in fear: "Jesus! Wake up! Don't you care that we are going to drown?" Jesus woke up and spoke over the water: "Silence! Be still!" The storm stopped immediately, and the water calmed down. Everything was peaceful, and the disciples could hardly believe what they had just witnessed. Even the wind and the waves obeyed Jesus!

Dear God, thank You for calming the storms around us. Help us to trust You when we are frightened by the chaos of life. Amen.

A Simple Prayer

This month, we are learning about patience. Jesus was patient when His disciples were terrified by the storm. When they woke Him up, He calmed the storm with just a few words. Jesus patiently taught His disciples about who He was and the power He had.

During September, pray this simple prayer with your family, thanking God for His patience with you!

Jesus, you are the perfect example of patience! Thank you for working in us to be steadfast and faithful. Teach us how to cultivate patience in our lives and in our relationships with one another. Help us to grow and serve you always. Amen.

September 26

Bible Verse of the Week

"Praise the lord from the earth, you creatures of the ocean depths, fire and hail, snow and clouds, wind and weather that obey him" (Psalm 148:7-8; NLT).

One of the best ways to grow personally and as a family is to memorize Scripture.

This week, we watched Jesus calm the storm. His power to bring peace to chaos was on full display. When He calmed the storm, He also calmed His disciples.

Take the time to memorize Psalm 148:7–8 with your family! Write it out and post it to your refrigerator. Let each person in your family have the opportunity to say it aloud, and then say it all together. Have fun enjoying the Word of God as a family!

Dear God, thank You for the Bible. Help us to memorize Your Word and to hide it in our hearts. Amen.

September 27

Do it!

Thunderstorms remind us of the power of nature. When it thunders loudly and when lightning strikes, we can feel our peace shaken. Storms can make us feel very small, especially if we are on a boat, surrounded by large waves and driving wind. We can end up just as frightened as the disciples were by the large storm that surrounded them.

Have you ever been in a big storm? Spend a few minutes writing down adjectives that describe the storm. Be as creative as possible. You can even use a thesaurus to find many different words to describe what you saw. Then take a large marker or crayon and write "Silence! Be still!" over top all the words.

Jesus calmed the wind and waves for the disciples. He will do the same for us when we ask. When we ask Him, He will bring us peace—sometimes by calming the chaotic situation, sometimes by calming us.

Dear God, You can calm the seas, and You can calm us. Thank You for being with us no matter what storm comes into our lives. Amen.

September 28

Talk About It

Over the last few weeks, we've read about Jesus' walking on water, sleeping through a storm, and calming the wind and the waves. Jesus had total authority over the sea and the sky. The disciples were consistently amazed by what He did and how He did it.

Think through both stories shared over the last few weeks about Jesus' walking on water and silencing the storm. Which situation took you by surprise and amazed you most? Why? Talk about your reactions with your family. Discuss how His power can calm the storm outside of us, as well as the storm within.

Talking about the miracles of Jesus always stirs our hearts to know Him better. We read Him doing the impossible throughout the New Testament. He has not changed! He still performs the impossible today. What a good Savior!

Dear Jesus, You are the master of the impossible! Help us to have faith in You and Your presence in our lives as we live through life's circumstances. Amen.

Serve One Another

Most likely, you won't be on a boat anytime soon, but you can still operate in faith the next time you encounter a storm. As autumn days overtake the warmth of summer, you'll most likely experience storms, complete with wind, rain, and lightning.

Make sure you are prepared for stormy days. Together with your family, put together a cozy day kit. Find coloring books and crayons, word game books, or even a jigsaw puzzle and put them in a handy place. Put a few packets of hot chocolate or cider nearby, along with a comfy blanket. When the storms roll in, settle in with one another and say a prayer, thanking God for shelter from the storm. Pray for safety, for the protection of people who are driving, and for the animals that may be outside. Remember to also thank God for giving you inner peace, even when storms rage.

Dear God, thank You for peace and safety. Help us to think of others during life's storms. Remind us to pray for them and help anyone in need of assistance. Amen.

September 30

Eat Together

This week, we read about Jesus calming the storm. He told the wind and waves to be silent and still, and they obeyed!

While discussing with your family what you learned this week in the Bible readings, make a batch of pancakes. Add some blue food coloring to the batter to make your pancakes the color of the sea. Stack them up high, as the waves around Jesus' boat rose up from the sea. Then pour your favorite syrup over the top. The syrup can remind you that Jesus' power "poured" peace over the wind and waves.

Pray with your family, thanking God for His faithful provision. Then finish your prayer with "Teach me to listen when You speak to my soul, "Silence. Be still." Then enjoy the tasty treat with your family. With each warm and gooey bite, thank Jesus for His life-changing miracles, both on the sea and at your kitchen table.

Dear God, thank You for good food to eat and for Your blessing over it. We are grateful that You calm us and provide for us. Amen.

The Great Physician

Matthew 9:18-26; Mark 5:21-43; Luke 8:40-56

Jesus and His disciples sailed through the storm and crossed the Sea of Galilee. When they reached the other side, people waited to greet Him.

One of them was a religious leader named Jairus. He had a very ill daughter, so he called out to Jesus, "Please help my little girl! She is very sick. Please come to my house and heal her." Jesus agreed and headed toward Jairus' home.

A massive number of people crowded around Him as He walked. As He made His way, a sick woman reached out to touch the hem of His robe. The moment she touched it, she felt better. Jesus knew what had happened and said to her, "Dear woman, the faith you have in Me has healed you."

Jesus continued to the house of Jairus; When they arrived at his home, the people were in mourning because the little girl had died. But Jesus said to Jairus, "Don't be afraid. Have faith. Your little girl is not dead. She is only sleeping." Jesus cleared the room and then went to the girl. He said, "Little girl, get up!" She woke up and started walking around. Everyone was astonished.

Dear God, You are the Great Physician. Thank You for showing us Your healing power. Help us to reach out to You when we are sick. Amen.

October 2

A Simple Prayer

This month, we are learning about remembrance. Remembering someone is to think of them or be reminded of them in some way. Jesus remembers us every day! We want to remember Him every day, too. Just as Jesus healed the woman and brought the little girl back to life, we can be remembered by Jesus in our everyday lives.

During October, pray this simple prayer with your family, thanking God for His remembrance of you!

Jesus, help us to remember You in all we do. Thank you for always remembering us and caring for us. Teach us how to receive You and cultivate remembrance in our lives and in our relationships with one another. Help us to grow and serve you always. Amen.

Bible Verse of the Week

"But if you remain in me and my words remain in you, you may ask for anything you want, and it will be granted!" (John 15:7; NLT).

One of the best ways to grow personally and as a family is to memorize Scripture.

This week, we learned how Jesus healed a woman and brought a girl back to life. His power over sickness and death was complete. It still is!

Take the time to memorize John 15:7 with your family! Write it out and post it to your refrigerator. Let each person in your family have the opportunity to say it aloud, and then say it all together. Have fun enjoying the Word of God as a family!

Dear God, thank You for the Bible. Help us to memorize Your Word and to hide it in our hearts. Amen.

October 4

Do it!

Praying is a wonderful way to remind ourselves of who God is when life's circumstances or struggles may make us doubt His power. We can feel hopeless or worrisome when we don't remember God's love for us. Have you ever felt any of these ways?

If you are going through a tough time or don't know what to pray, Jesus gave us these words. They are called the Lord's Prayer, and they help us remember who God is and what He can do. It is found in Matthew 6:9–13 NIV.

> Our Father in heaven,
> Hallowed be your name,
> Your kingdom come,
> Your will be done,
> On earth as it is in heaven.
> Give us today our daily bread.
> And forgive us our debts,
> As we also have forgiven our debtors.
> And lead us not into temptation,
> But deliver us from the evil one.

Say this prayer every day for a whole week and see how your life changes!

Dear God, thank You for providing us with The Lord's Prayer. Be with us as we remember Your gift of life. Amen.

Talk About It

Prayer is bringing our needs to God and connecting with Him. Even though God knows our needs before we speak them, talking to Him is important. He loves to hear from us, and He wants to spend time with us.

What in your life do you need to take to God in prayer? Is there something you're struggling with? Do you or someone you know suffer from an illness? God wants to know. Do you have any friends or family who may be going through a tough time and could use a couple prayers to bring comfort and care?

Today, talk with God about any problem in your life or the lives of those you love. Ask Him to bring His love and healing into each situation.

Dear God, help us remember to reach out to you when we need something. You are a good Father who loves helping Your children. Amen.

October 6

Serve One Another

When people get sick or older, they often need attention and care. Sometimes, they need to spend long periods of time at the hospital or a nursing home. Bringing small gifts to cheer up patients is a kind and loving way to show them care.

Is there a hospital or nursing home near you? Ask your parents to give them a call and find out how you can care for the patients there. They might allow you to visit and spend a few minutes talking to the sick or elderly. By spending a little time with people who need physical care, you show them that you remember them in their time of need. It is a generous, loving, and kind thing to do so.

Dear God, Remind me to look for simple ways to care and connect with people who are sick or older. Help me be a blessing to those who may need cheered up or for a friend to simply stop by.
Amen.

Eat Together

Sometimes, we live through sour patches of time—times when life is hard. When life is tough, we can always prepare a snack that makes us laugh. Try making these sour patch grapes with your family. You'll need 1.5 lbs. of green grapes, half a lemon, two teaspoons of citric acid, and 3-ounce packages of cherry, orange, lemon, and lime Jell-o™.

Open all flavors of Jell-o™ and empty each into a separate gallon-sized, plastic bag. To each bag, add one half teaspoon one of citric acid. Rinse and dry the grapes, then squeeze lemon juice on them until covered. Put one handful of grapes inside each bag of mix, and shake.

Pour each bag into an individual bowl and enjoy while discussing what you learned this week about The Great Physician.

Dear God, thank You for Your great love. Help us to remember to talk to You when life gets tough. Amen.

Let Them Come
Matthew 19:14; Mark 10:13-15

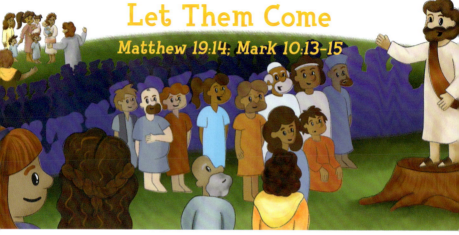

Jesus spent much time with His disciples teaching them and training them. They saw most of Jesus' miracles, and they had the opportunity to witness His ministry firsthand.

People heard about all Jesus was doing, and they started to bring their children so He would pray for them. The disciples didn't want the children to bother Jesus, and they rebuked them. Jesus was upset because He loved spending time with kids. He said, "Let the little children come to me, and do not hinder them, for the kingdom of God belongs to such as these. Truly I tell you, anyone who will not receive the kingdom of God like a little child will never enter it."

Jesus prayed for the little children and held them in His arms.

Dear Jesus, You say to come to you with the faith of a child. We ask that You remind us that we are Your children. Help us to be humble in heart and to have the purity of a child to see You as You are. Amen.

October 9

A Simple Prayer

This month, we are learning about remembrance.

This week, we learned how Jesus remembered the little children, even when the disciples thought He wouldn't want to be bothered by them. We can listen to and care for the little children around us as we try to be like them—humble and trusting.

During October, pray this simple prayer with your family, thanking God for His remembrance of you!

Jesus, help us to remember You in all we do. Thank you for always remembering us and caring for us. Teach us how to receive You and cultivate remembrance in our lives and in our relationships with one another. Help us to grow and serve you always. Amen.

Bible Verse of the Week

"So anyone who becomes as humble as this little child is the greatest in the Kingdom of Heaven" (Matthew 18:4, NLT).

One of the best ways to grow personally and as a family is to memorize Scripture.

This week, we watched Jesus love and welcome the little children. He loves those who come to Him with such humility and trust.

Take the time to memorize Matthew 18:4 with your family! Write it out and post it to your refrigerator. Let each person in your family have the opportunity to say it aloud, and then say it all together. Have fun enjoying the Word of God as a family!

Dear God, thank You for the Bible. Help us to memorize Your Word and to hide it in our hearts. Amen.

October 11

Do it!

Do you know any little children? Likely, you have siblings or friends, cousins or neighbors who are younger than you. What do you enjoy about spending time with children? Are they cute, fun to play with, or innocent like babies?

Jesus loved spending time with kids. Children tend to be very honest, live in the present moment, and love to be active. Take the opportunity today to spend some time with a person who is younger than you. Play a game or read a book. Comfort a baby or child when they cry or even help feed one.

By loving the little children, you live like Jesus. By serving those who need someone to watch over them, you show that you value and care for them.

Dear God, thank You for the little children. Help us to serve with care those who are younger than we. Amen.

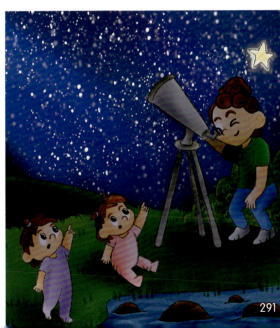

Talk About It

Our Bible verse this week teaches us to be humble like little children. When we are humble, we are more like Jesus.

Do you know what humble means? Discuss this with your family before you continue.

To be humble means to be respectful of others and consider others as more important than yourself. It is the opposite of being puffed up with pride. Little children are often humble because they take instructions from adults and need the help of people older. Children are learning simple life tasks, and are happy to be taught. Jesus says this is what the Kingdom is all about!

Is there anyone in your life that you consider to be humble? Why do you consider them humble? Are you humble? Why or why not?

Talk about humility with your family today and write down a few ways you can practice being humble and respectful to others.

Dear God, please help us learn humility in all we do. We don't want to be puffed up with pride; we want to learn the ways of Your Kingdom. Amen.

October 13

Serve One Another

Children are a gift of God. Jesus thought highly of them and liked to spend time with them. He knew that serving little ones was a way to honor His Father. The disciples mistakenly thought He would rather do something else. Jesus chose to teach children while being followed by crowds of adults. It was clear He truly loved to serve all people.

Have you ever thought of volunteering to help out with the kids at church? Even if you aren't old enough to help out on your own, perhaps you could serve alongside your mom or dad. Serving in kids' church is a wonderful way to watch God at work and to serve others in His name.

If serving at church isn't an option, you could offer to babysit during a small group or watch over a neighborhood child at the playground. No matter where you serve kids, know that you are doing God's work!

Dear God, help me see life through the eyes of children. Show me how to have faith like a small child. Amen.

October 14

Eat Together

Serving kids always includes snacks! And when you serve snacks to little kids, you must make sure the snack is cut up into bite-sized pieces. You don't want them to get choked! When dealing with little ones, everything should be in small pieces, including Bible lessons. Simplified lessons break everything down so that even little ones can hear about Jesus in a way they will understand.

What kind of snacks do you see kids eat? Go with your family today and pick up some fresh produce, like strawberries or bananas; maybe even get some cheese. Practice cutting the fruit and cheese into small bites, perfect for a little mouth to enjoy. Have your mom or dad help you, so you know the size is just right.

Then, enjoy eating your bite-sized snacks as a family. While you eat, discuss all the reasons Jesus enjoyed the company of children.

Dear Jesus, help us to remember to serve the little kids we encounter. Show us how to care for them and nurture them as you do. Amen.

The Widow's Offering
Mark 12:38-44; Luke 21:1-4

October 15

One day, Jesus sat near the temple offering boxes. While watching people drop their money gifts into the offering, He noticed a rich man put in a large number of coins. The coins made noise as they fell; likely, the man hoped everyone would hear and know the size of his donation and think highly of him as a result.

Next, a poor woman walked up and dropped two coins in the box. Her offering would be worth about a penny today. She had lost everything when her husband died, and the two coins were all she had left. Jesus honored her sacrifice when He said, "Did you see that woman? What I tell you is true. She put more into the offering than anybody else. The amount the rich man gave was tiny compared to all the money he has left. But the woman, even though she is poor, put in everything she had."

Dear God, help us remember this poor woman's generosity. Remind us that You see our hearts and prefer humility over large sums put in an offering box. Amen.

A Simple Prayer

This month, we are learning about remembrance.

Jesus honored the poor woman's offering more than the abundant amounts given by the wealthy. He saw the pure love with which her tiny offering was given and the faith it took for her to part with the only money she possessed.

We can be faithful with our money, no matter the amount. We should remember that Jesus considers the attitude of our hearts to be of much more value than money.

During October, pray this simple prayer with your family, thanking God for His remembrance of you!

Jesus, help us to remember You in all we do. Thank you for always remembering us and caring for us. Teach us how to receive You and cultivate remembrance in our lives and in our relationships with one another. Help us to grow and serve you always. Amen.

Bible Verse of the Week

One of the best ways to grow personally and as a family is to memorize Scripture.

This week, we learned how Jesus honored a poor woman when she placed her last two coins in the offering. He saw her heart and knew she gave out of love and trust for God.

Take the time to memorize 1 Timothy 6:17 with your family! Write it out and post it to your refrigerator. Let each person in your family have the opportunity to say it aloud, and then say it all together. Have fun enjoying the Word of God as a family!

Dear God, thank You for the Bible. Help us to memorize Your Word and to hide it in our hearts. Amen.

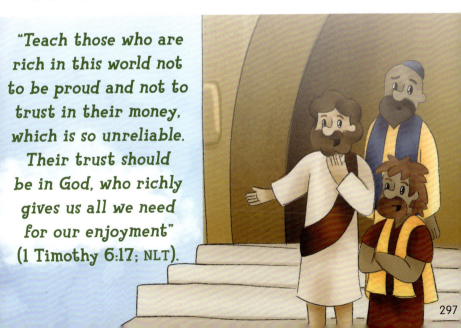

"Teach those who are rich in this world not to be proud and not to trust in their money, which is so unreliable. Their trust should be in God, who richly gives us all we need for our enjoyment" (1 Timothy 6:17; NLT).

October 18

Do it!

Unlike the woman in the story, most of us have more than we need. We may get prideful when we give, thinking we should receive some kind of praise or honor. If so, we do not understand giving at all.

The widow gave all she had, even though it was a small amount, Jesus was blessed by her gift. She gave everything she had without holding back, showing how much she loved God.

Discuss with your family what it would be like to give away all you have.

As a family, spend time going through your home and closets. Find items that can be donated to a homeless shelter or to an organization that helps others. Give freely to those who may have nothing. As you do, say a prayer for the people who will receive what you are giving, Thank God for each of them and ask Him to bless their lives.

Dear God, show me how to be generous with my life and my things. Help me remember to bless others and be faithful to You with my resources. Amen.

Talk About It

God takes care of us all the time, even when we don't recognize it. Paying attention to the blessings we have is a wonderful way to honor God. It helps us slow down and give thanks for the things we may take for granted. It will help us remember to be generous with all the Lord has provided. We can be like the poor woman who used her resources to honor God, and Jesus Himself honored her. What a blessing to witness!

Make a list of all the ways you have noticed God's generosity in your life. How has He provided for you? Have there been any moments recently when you gave Jesus all that you had?

Spend today talking with your family about all the wonderful ways God has taken care of you. Celebrate His life and goodness and remind each other to be thankful at all times.

Dear God, You are wonderful. Thank You for being so generous with us. Remind us to give our gifts back to You. Amen.

October 20

Serve One Another

Do you know any widows or widowers? A widow or widower is a person whose spouse has passed away. It can feel very lonely when your partner and best friend is no longer with you every day. God asks us to care for widows in their distress, which means that we should look out for ways to help men and women who have lost the love of their lives.

Consider any widows or widowers in your life. If there is one nearby, perhaps you could rake their leaves for them or bring them a plate of cookies. If you don't know anyone personally, perhaps you could send a handwritten note card, or small gift to someone at an assisted living center or nursing home where there are likely many who have lost a husband or wife.

Whoever you choose to serve, remember to mention them in your prayers. In doing so, you also honor God.

Dear God, remind me to think of widows and widowers in their distress. Help me to show care to those who may be lonely or in need of a helping hand. Amen.

October 21

Eat Together

Kids typically love chicken nuggets. They are a staple of childhood. If you could suddenly never have chicken nuggets again, would you be sad? Most likely you would!

Just like the widow put in her small coins, which was everything she had, consider what it might be like to share your very last chicken nuggets, knowing there were no more. Coins and chicken nuggets are very different; but the concept of giving away is the last of what you have is the same whether it's money or food.

Cook some chicken nuggets today with your family and talk about the widow's story as you prepare them. Thank God that He provides both coins and chicken nuggets to show us that He remembers to provide for all His children. Bless your food and share it with your family around the table.

Dear God, thank You for food to eat. Remind us to be grateful and give to others as a way to honor You. Amen.

The Lamb of God

October 22

Matthew 26:17-29; Mark 14:12-25; Luke 22:7-20; John 13:1-20

Passover is a traditional celebration for the Jewish people. It began when Israel was enslaved by Egypt. God sent Moses to tell Pharaoh to let the Israelites leave. Pharaoh wouldn't, so God sent plagues to convince him. The last one was the plague of death. On this day, God told Israel to put the blood of a lamb over the doors of their houses so that the plague of death would pass over their homes. From that day, Jewish people have had special meals to celebrate God saving His people from death.

Passover was near and Jesus knew it was nearly His time to die on the cross. He wanted to share a Passover meal with His disciples. He began by washing His disciples' feet. He explained that this was to remind them that His purpose for existing was to serve those around Him and give up His life for them.

Afterward, they sat down to eat and Jesus explained that He was going to die soon. All of the disciples were very sad. Jesus raised a loaf of bread, thanked God, and said, "This is My body that is broken for you. Take and eat. Every time you do, remember Me." He then raised a cup of wine and said, "This is My blood that will be poured out to forgive the sins of many. Take and drink. Every time you do, remember Me."

Dear God, thank You for the gift of Jesus, the Passover Lamb. Help us to remember Him always and give thanks for how He has saved us. Amen.

October 23

A Simple Prayer

This month we are learning about remembrance. Before Jesus served His followers the loaf of bread and before He passed the cup of wine, He said "Do this in remembrance of me." When He shared His Last Supper with His disciples, Jesus taught how to honor Him and the sacrifice He offers for each of us.

During October, pray this simple prayer with your family, thanking God for His remembrance of you!

Jesus, help us to remember You in all we do. Thank you for always remembering us and caring for us. Teach us how to receive You and cultivate remembrance in our lives and in our relationships with one another. Help us to grow and serve you always. Amen.

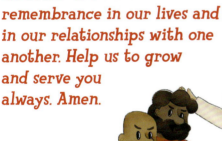

Bible Verse of the Week

"The next day John [the Baptist] saw Jesus coming toward him and said, 'Look! The Lamb of God who takes away the sin of the world!'" (John 1:29; NLT).

One of the best ways to grow personally and as a family is to memorize Scripture.

This week, we learned about Jesus and the Last Supper. Jesus told His followers to remember Him every time the bread and wine were shared in His name. He was talking to us as well as the ones who sat at the table with Him.

Take the time to memorize John 1:29 with your family! Write it out and post it to your refrigerator. Let each person in your family have the opportunity to say it aloud, and then say it all together. Have fun enjoying the Word of God as a family!

Dear God, thank You for the Bible. Help us to memorize Your Word and to hide it in our hearts. Amen.

October 25

Do it!

Many churches serve Communion; it is also known as the Last Supper. Communion is the tradition Jesus taught His followers to help them remember Him and His gift of salvation. Still, today, we pause and remember the sacrifice of Jesus when we take Communion or celebrate the Last Supper.

Does your church serve Communion? Have you ever asked your mom or dad about taking Communion? Have you talked about Communion with a pastor or priest at your church?

Now is a great time to ask your parents about celebrating Communion at church. Ask them to share with you how old they were when they started taking communion. Ask if they have any stories about Communion from when they were children?

Dear God, thank You for the celebration of Communion. Help us understand Your gift of salvation through this powerful tradition. Amen.

Talk About It

Whether we call it Communion or the Last Supper, this is a time set aside for remembrance. We recall how Jesus took our sin upon Himself, died in our place, and gave us new life. By sitting down and reflecting on His good gift, we can also pause and take a few minutes to think about how we live our lives.

Is there anything in your life you struggle with and can't seem to overcome? Jesus can help. Is there a sinful act or attitude you need to confess to God? Jesus can be there with you. Is there anything you need to apologize for or make right? Jesus wants to know that, too.

As we reflect on what has distracted us from Jesus, we can repent and ask for His help to change. Talk with your family today about a few of the struggles you may have. Ask them to pray for you, and you can pray for them, too!

Dear God, thank You for dying on the cross, coming back to life, and giving us new life in You. Help us to remember to pause and reflect often. Amen.

October 27

Serve One Another

Jesus is a true servant. Even at the Last Supper, He was serving His disciples at the meal and washing their feet. When we live our lives according to the example we see in Jesus, we can honor others and be generous, as He was.

Can you think of a few ways you can honor and serve your family members today? Perhaps you can take out the trash without being asked. Maybe you can pick up items lying around the house and put them away. You may decide to set the table for dinner or help your parents put laundry away. There are so many ways to serve and honor others!

Be purposefully kind to your parents and siblings and be a good example to those around you. Serving others doesn't have to be complicated, it can be very simple. By doing the little things well, you show the love of Jesus to those around you.

Dear God, thank You for serving Your children. Help us remember that Jesus is the perfect example of honoring You and others. Amen.

Eat Together

Grapes, in some form, are one of the main ingredients in Communion (or Last Supper). Whether you use wine or grape juice, both are made by crushing the juice from grapes.

Grapes come in many forms and colors—there are red grapes, purple grapes, and green grapes. You can also find grape juice that is purple or a yellowish white. There are white and purple raisins, both are dried grapes.

You may have grapes in some form already in your home. If not, go to the store and browse around. Discover the variety of this sweet fruit that is available. Take home some grapes in one or more forms to enjoy as a snack.

While you eat or drink your grapes, talk with your family about what you learned this week regarding Jesus and the Last Supper.

Dear God, help us to remember You in big ways and in little ways. We want to always live our lives for You. Amen.

October 29

A Lonely Night in the Garden
Matthew 26:30, 36-56; Mark 14:26, 32-52; Luke 22:39-53; John 18:1-12

After celebrating Passover, Jesus and the disciples walked to the Mount of Olives. Jesus wanted to have time alone to pray, as He was feeling very sad and overwhelmed. He knew the time for Him to die was coming quickly. When they entered the Garden of Gethsemane, Jesus asked Peter, James, and John to stay awake and keep watch while He prayed.

Jesus prayed, "Father, everything is possible for You. I do not want to suffer, but I will do what You want, not what I want." An angel came to strengthen Him as He prayed. He went to check on Peter, James, and John and found them sleeping. He woke them up and asked them, again, to stay awake while He continued to pray. Jesus checked on them twice more, and both times they were sleeping. They were embarrassed.

Then, Judas appeared with an angry crowd of religious leaders and soldiers. He kissed Jesus on the cheek; this was to inform the religious leaders which man was Jesus. The soldiers grabbed Jesus. Peter was upset and cut off the ear of one of the men. Jesus told Peter to stop and then healed the man's ear. Jesus was taken away by the soldiers and His disciples all ran away. Jesus knew beforehand exactly what they would do.

Dear God, help us to remember to pray to You when we are sad. Just like Jesus, help us to be brave while doing Your will. Amen.

A Simple Prayer

This month we are learning about remembrance. When Jesus prayed in the Garden of Gethsemane, He was remembering His Father's will. When we pause and pray to God, for strength to follow through on His instructions, we remind ourselves that He is the One who is in control. Even when situations are difficult, when we do as God asks, He will give us strength and peace.

During October, pray this simple prayer with your family, thanking God for His remembrance of you!

Jesus, help us to remember You in all we do. Thank you for always remembering us and caring for us. Teach us how to receive You and cultivate remembrance in our lives and in our relationships with one another. Help us to grow and serve you always. Amen.

October 31

Bible Verse of the Week

"The lord is close to the brokenhearted; he rescues those whose spirits are crushed" (Psalm 34:18, NLT).

One of the best ways to grow personally and as a family is to memorize Scripture.

This week, we learned about Jesus praying in the Garden of Gethsemane. He asked God to help Him face the most difficult time in His life. We can be sure, God will also be with us when we face difficult or sorrowful times.

Take the time to memorize Psalm 34:18 with your family! Write it out and post it to your refrigerator. Let each person in your family have the opportunity to say it aloud, and then say it all together. Have fun enjoying the Word of God as a family!

Dear God, thank You for the Bible. Help us to memorize Your Word and to hide it in our hearts. Amen.

November 1

Do it!

Have you ever been in a situation that made you so sad that you didn't know what to do? Jesus was overwhelmed with sorrow because He knew that His time on earth was over and He would soon die a cruel death. Even though Jesus did not want to experience the pain and heartbreak of the cross, He knew that it was His Father's will that He do so.

Jesus was very brave to follow through, even though He could have stopped the road to the cross at any time. He knew, though, that His death would provide the way for each of us to be saved. Jesus' death provides new life for anyone who will repent and put full faith in Jesus' sacrifice. Jesus considered death to be a necessary price to pay to bring new life to any who would believe in Him.

Find a quiet place, maybe outdoors, and spend a few minutes in prayer. If it is too cold outside, find a cozy place indoors to curl up and reflect on what Jesus did for You. Thank Him for His gift and for His sacrifice, knowing that He loves you more than you can imagine!

Dear Jesus, thank You for saving us and for enduring the cross. Remind us of all You have done for us and make us truly grateful. Amen.

November 2

Talk About It

There are many times throughout the New Testament that tell us Jesus went off alone to pray to His Father. He often went away from the crowd to be with God and talk to Him. Jesus knew that connection with God would enable Him to serve His Father faithfully.

Do you often talk to God when you are overwhelmed or need a break?

We may be tempted to hide the way we feel when we are sad. We may stay super busy or spend far too much time on phones. We will often do anything to keep from thinking about difficult things we face.

Admitting our hearts hurt and bringing our concerns to God can feel painful at the time; but talking things out with Him bring comfort and give us strength.

Talk these things out with your family:
   Why do you think God wants us to pray?
   Share with one another ways you cope with being sad.
   What are healthy ways to handle sadness?
   What are a few unhealthy ways to be sad?

Dear God, You are our example of all the right ways to live. Even when you struggled, you found comfort and strength through prayer. Help us to be like You. Amen.

November 3

Serve One Another

When Jesus went alone to the garden to pray, He asked specific friends to stay close by and keep watch. While He spoke to His Father about His breaking heart, He wanted His disciples to be alert and aware of what was happening around them.

When you are going through a hard time, do you have close friends and family that you call? Perhaps you ask your mom or dad to listen to your problem or give you a hug. Maybe you even have them sit with you, or cuddle with them for a little while. Loved ones were important to Jesus. He loved His disciples, and He loves us!

Make a list of friends and family who you can call to have close by if you need extra prayers or support. Also list ways you can be a friend who is available for anyone who needs your prayers or support. It's important for all of us to stay awake and alert on behalf of one another, especially those who might be working through something difficult or sad.

Dear God, thank You for being the best friend there is! Help me to be a good and available friend to others. Amen.

November 4

Eat Together

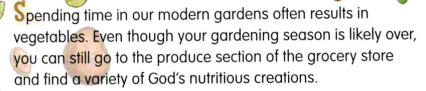

Spending time in our modern gardens often results in vegetables. Even though your gardening season is likely over, you can still go to the produce section of the grocery store and find a variety of God's nutritious creations.

Take a trip to the grocery store with your family. Choose three or four vegetables you can chop up for soup. Be creative and try to find some flavors that might be fun to put together. Then locate your favorite flavor of broth and choose two cartons.

Once you are home, heat the broth while chopping the veggies into bite-sized pieces. Add the veggies to the boiling broth, along with seasonings of your choice. Let the veggies boil on medium heat until tender. Serve with crackers or cheese and enjoy!

While you eat, share with your family what you learned from this week's reading. Thank God for the nourishment He has provided. Talk with your family about how God will nourish our souls, as well as our bodies. He will strengthen and comfort us just as He did for Jesus on the night He was betrayed. The Garden of Gethsemane was a place of sorrow for Him; but it was also a place of prayer and promise.

Dear God, thank You for the joy of praying and being with You, no matter the circumstances. We love You. Amen.

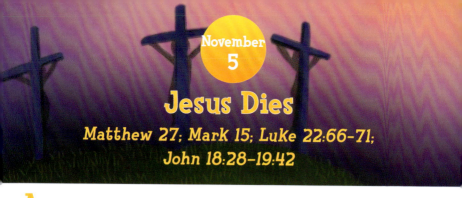

Jesus Dies

Matthew 27; Mark 15; Luke 22:66-71; John 18:28-19:42

After Jesus was taken from the Garden of Gethsemane, He was brought before the high priest, Caiaphas, and the other religious leaders. They asked Him if he was the Messiah, God's Son. Jesus told them He was. The leaders offered to release Jesus, but the people shouted, "Crucify Him!" saying he claimed to be the King of the Jews which was a capital crime. The leaders then whipped Him and ordered Him to be put to death by hanging on a cross. They mocked Him, and put a purple robe on Him. They made Him a crown of thorns and pushed it into His head. With cruelness, they exclaimed: "Hail, the King of the Jews!"

Jesus carried part of a heavy cross all the way through the trails and streets of Jerusalem until He reached the hill outside the city called Golgotha. There, Jesus' hands and feet were nailed to the cross. While He was dying in agony, He cried out, "My God, My God, why have you left Me?" Then at the very end, Jesus said, "It is finished." The Son of God who had complete power, willingly died. His body was wrapped in cloth and laid inside a tomb. A large stone was placed in the opening and guards were ordered to watch through the night so no one stole His body.

Dear God, thank You for dying for us on the cross. Help us to remember what You've done for us and never take it for granted. Amen.

November 6

A Simple Prayer

This month, we are learning about gratitude. We can be full of gratitude for what Jesus did on our behalf. By dying on the cross, He made a way for us to receive eternal life and live with Him forever. We can thank Jesus every day for this special gift.

During November, pray this simple prayer with your family, expressing gratitude for all God has done for you.

Jesus, we are so grateful for You! Thank You for filling our hearts and inviting us into Your presence. Teach us how to cultivate gratitude in our lives and in our relationships with one another. Help us to grow and serve you always. Amen.

November 7

Bible Verse of the Week

Christ died for our sins. He took our sin upon Himself and then paid our death penalty. His death paid the penalty for all people for all time. He suffered physical death, but three days later, He was raised to life in the Spirit. (1 Peter 3:18.)

One of the best ways to grow personally and as a family is to memorize Scripture.

This week, we learned about Jesus dying on the cross for our sins. He paid the penalty for our sin, which was death, so that we could be with Him forever.

Take the time to memorize 1 Peter 3:18 with your family! Write it out and post it to your refrigerator. Let each person in your family have the opportunity to say it aloud, and then say it all together. Have fun enjoying the Word of God as a family!

Dear God, thank You for the Bible. Help us to memorize Your Word and to hide it in our hearts. Amen.

November 8

Do it!

Many churches and communities exhibit the stations of the cross around Easter time. Typically, these are a series of scenes that depict what Jesus experienced before, during, and after His death on Golgotha. At each depicted scene, a prayer is suggested to thank Jesus for all He did on behalf of mankind. Some churches keep the stations of the cross available to view and pray through all year round. Do you know of a local church where you can see the stations this time of year?

If not, your parents can research the stations and go over each one with you. Remembering these steps helps us be grateful for the details of the crucifixion. We can get very busy in our lives and forget to ponder exactly what Jesus has done on our behalf.

Consider the stations of the cross today, and spend time being with Jesus.

Dear God, Your death on the cross is so difficult to consider, but the love it displays is so very beautiful. Thank You. We are grateful. Amen.

Talk About It

The day we recognize Jesus' death on the cross is referred to as Good Friday. It can feel anything but "good" because Jesus endured so much pain and sorrow. Jesus' purpose on Earth was to bridge the gap that sin created between God and humans. He paid our penalty and enabled us to be reconciled to God by accepting His sacrifice on our behalf. He then inhabits our hearts, giving us the ability to follow through with His instructions to live as He commands.

It's important to remember Good Friday because we sometimes need to pause and simply be grateful. We can lose sight of the price Jesus paid for us when we go about our busy lives. We should never take for granted the good gift Jesus gave us.

Spend a few minutes with your family today discussing all the reasons it is important to think about Good Friday, in all its sorrow. Talk with your family about ways your family can remember and honor Good Friday each year.

Dear God, the day of Your death is an awful day; but the love You displayed is beyond beautiful. Help us to embrace the reality of what You have done for us and be forever grateful. Amen.

November 10

Serve One Another

Good Friday is the perfect day to remember those who suffer on behalf of the Gospel. Have you ever heard of missionaries or the underground church? In certain places in the world, people are not allowed to be Christians. If they are, they can be beaten, hurt, or wounded, just as Jesus when He was beaten and crucified.

If a person becomes a Christian in these parts of the world, his or her family often disowns them. Following Jesus in these areas can be extremely dangerous. Oftentimes, these Christians must meet and worship in secret, hiding from the world to serve the Lord. When discovered, they may be beaten, imprisoned, or even killed. This is called persecution.

We can support the persecuted church by praying for them and sending resources like money or Bibles. Look up a few organizations that help Christians in areas of the world where Christianity is unlawful. Your pastor will likely know of a few. Send a donation, if you can, and pray for people who are living as persecuted.

Dear God, please protect Christians who are in danger in other countries. Show us how we can support and care for them in practical ways. Amen.

Eat Together

Everyone dislikes some kinds of food. Sometimes, foods that taste the worst to us actually contain nourishment that our bodies need to be healthy. Have your parents ever told you to eat your vegetables?

Each person in the family should find one vegetable in the house (or grocery store) they dislike. Sit at the table as a family and let everyone have a turn taking a bite of something they don't like. Those who are persecuted for their faith, often have little to eat. The food you dislike could be life saving for them. Our minor displeasures are very manageable in comparison to the sorrow our persecuted brothers and sisters are living through. See if you can follow through with swallowing your least favorite vegetable. Talk with your family about how it tasted like. Practice being grateful for the freedoms God has given you. Remember to pray for those who are fighting to survive in much worse conditions.

Dear God, thank You for allowing us to be born in a country where we are allowed to worship You. Help us to be mindful of Your extreme blessing in our lives. Amen.

November 12
Jesus is Alive!
Matthew 28:1-15

Jesus died on Good Friday. His body was buried in a borrowed tomb and a massive stone was rolled over the opening.

On Sunday, Mary Magdalene and some other women went to the tomb. Suddenly, an earthquake shook the ground and the stone that sealed the tomb rolled away! The guards were terrified, and the women ran into the tomb. There, they found an angel sitting on the stone that had covered the opening to the tomb. The angel said, "Don't be afraid. I know you are looking for Jesus who was crucified. But He is not here! He is risen from the dead!" (Matthew 28:5–6, NLT).

The women were scared and amazed. They hurried to tell the disciples what had happened. On their way, Jesus appeared to them. He said, "Don't be afraid! Go tell my brothers to leave for Galilee, and they will see me there" (Matthew 28:10; NLT).

The women told the disciples all they had seen and what Jesus had said, but none of the disciples believed their story. Peter and John even ran to the tomb and couldn't believe his eyes. The cloths that had covered Jesus' face and body were folded and laying there, but Jesus' body was gone!

That very evening, Jesus' disciples were hiding out in a locked room. Suddenly, Jesus appeared as if from nowhere! He greeted His friends by saying, "Peace be with you!" Everyone was overjoyed.

Dear God, thank You for overcoming death and giving us life. You are the best miracle ever. Amen.

A Simple Prayer

This month, we are learning about gratitude.

After Jesus rose from the dead, He went to visit His friends. They were astounded to see Him! Once they realized Jesus had truly risen from death, they were full of gratitude for all Jesus had done.

We can also be full of gratitude as we thank God for Jesus and His victory over sin and death.

During November, pray this simple prayer with your family, expressing gratitude for all God has done for you.

Jesus, we are so grateful for You! Thank You for filling our hearts and inviting us into Your presence. Teach us how to cultivate gratitude in our lives and in our relationships with one another. Help us to grow and serve you always. Amen.

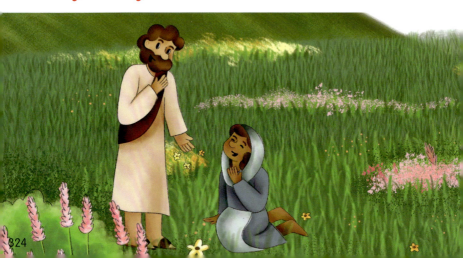

Bible Verse of the Week

"Then the angel spoke to the women. 'Don't be afraid!' he said. 'I know you are looking for Jesus, who was crucified. He isn't here! He is risen from the dead, just as He said would happen'" (Matthew 28:5-6; NLT).

One of the best ways to grow personally and as a family is to memorize Scripture.

This week we read about Jesus returning to life after being crucified and buried. It is His resurrection (rising from death) that is the foundation of all we believe. He died so we don't have to; then He rose again, proving death could not hold Him! Jesus holds total power over sin and the grave!

Take the time to memorize Matthew 28:5–6 with your family! Write it out and post it to your refrigerator. Let each person in your family have the opportunity to say it aloud, and then say it all together. Have fun enjoying the Word of God as a family!

Dear God, thank You for the Bible. Help us to memorize Your Word and to hide it in our hearts. Amen.

November 15

Do it!

Have you ever been so tired that it was difficult to wake up in the morning? It may be that you stayed up late the night before, or you spent a lot of energy playing. It can be tough to wake up after you've been really active or after you have worked really hard.

When you go to sleep tonight (or another day this week), set an alarm to wake you before sunrise. As you get up, imagine how it might have felt to be Jesus waking in the dark tomb. Since you're up early, grab your Bible and read the resurrection story in Matthew 28. Then, before your day begins, go to the Lord in prayer and thank Him for all He's done.

Celebrate the gift of new mercies each morning, including the victory we know every day because Jesus rose from the dead!

Dear Jesus, we celebrate You! We want to live like You. We want to love like You. Amen.

Talk About It

The story of Jesus' death and resurrection is often read on Easter, the day set aside by Christians to celebrate Jesus' amazing gift to us.

Easter is celebrated in a variety of fun ways! It always happens in the spring when the sun is warm, flowers are growing, and grass and leaves turn vibrant green. You will see a lot of decorations with chicks and bunnies as some people's way of celebrating Easter. Families often color eggs for kids and just about everyone eats a little bit more chocolate than usual.

Does your family have any Easter celebration traditions? What are they? What is the reason behind your traditions? How do they celebrate the new life of Jesus in your heart?

Talk with your family about Easter. Now that you have read through the story of Jesus' resurrection, try to come up with new ways of celebrating that remind you of why Easter is celebrated at all.

Dear God, we love celebrating You! Help us to walk in faith and new life in everything we do. Amen.

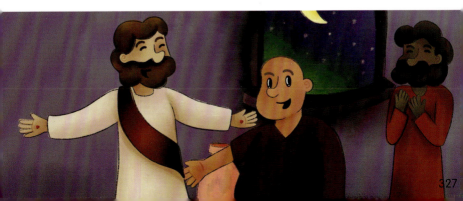

November 17

Serve One Another

As we grow in our relationships with Jesus, we are better able to treat others with the love and kindness He brings us in our new lives in Him. Just as Jesus always helps us live as God desires, we can do the same for others.

Are you good at something that is difficult for one of your family members? Is one of your siblings good at something that you hate doing? Spend today helping one another out! If there is a chore you love to do, do it without seeking repayment. If your mom, sibling, or friend are good at a certain skill, let them teach you without interrupting them. Living in a giving and receiving community while sharing our gifts with one another, allows us to live out the new life Jesus gave us. It is good to share what we have and what we know with each other! It helps us grow and experience Jesus in new ways.

Dear God, help us to serve one another with full hearts and blessed minds. Help us learn and grow together. Amen.

November 18

Eat Together

This is a week of celebration! Because Jesus was crucified and rose from death, we can be transformed and know an amazing new life.

Spend today gathering a few of your family's favorite foods. Have each person choose a side dish they love, a main dish they always enjoy, or a favorite sweet dessert. Combine your choices into a meal to enjoy together.

While experiencing the sweet and savory flavors of your foods, talk about what it must have been like for the friends of Jesus when He appeared to them after His death. What a gift! He defeated sin, rose from the dead, and then blessed His people. He is still blessing His people today. Jesus gives us fullness of life in every way.

Be blessed today as you share in all the goodness and joy of your favorite dishes and celebrate the One who makes all things new.

Dear Jesus, You are worthy to be celebrated and honored! Thank You for defeating sin and death and always giving us good gifts to enjoy. Amen.

November 19

The Good News
Matthew 28:16-20

After Jesus rose from the dead, He spent forty days on Earth visiting His friends. He told them to tell everyone about Him so that all people could find new life in Him. He explained that because He would live within them, all His followers have authority to share the Good News and make even more disciples.

He told them to baptize believers in the name of the Father, and the Son, and the Holy Spirit, and teach them to do everything as He did. He promised He would be with them forever. (See Matthew 28:18–20.)

Because the disciples had spent much time watching Jesus do good works on Earth, they knew His great love could change lives and His power brought forth miracles. They loved Jesus, and they wanted to do what He instructed them to do.

Dear God, help us share the Good News with those around us. We want to love others and offer them new life, just as You did. Amen.

A Simple Prayer

This month, we are learning about gratitude.

When we look back on the life of Jesus, we see all the love He shared and all the good works He performed on behalf of people. He did many miracles, healed the sick, and shared about His Father. After His resurrection, He told everyone to share the Good News about Him.

This November, pray this simple prayer with your family, expressing gratitude for all God has done for you.

Jesus, we are so grateful for You! Thank You for filling our hearts and inviting us into Your presence. Teach us how to cultivate gratitude in our lives and in our relationships with one another. Help us to grow and serve you always. Amen.

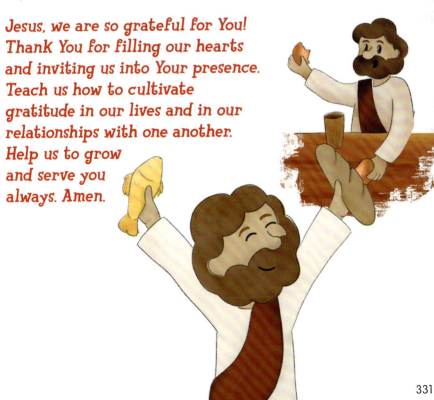

November 21

Bible Verse of the Week

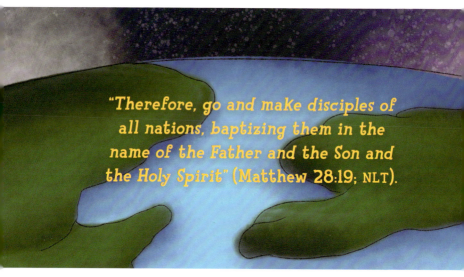

"Therefore, go and make disciples of all nations, baptizing them in the name of the Father and the Son and the Holy Spirit" (Matthew 28:19; NLT).

One of the best ways to grow personally and as a family is to memorize Scripture.

This week in our reading, we learned that Jesus told His followers to share the Good News with the world. He wants all people to know about His love, His sacrifice, and His gift of new life that is available to everyone.

Take the time to memorize Matthew 28:19 with your family! Write it out and post it to your refrigerator. Let each person in your family have the opportunity to say it aloud, and then say it all together. Have fun enjoying the Word of God as a family!

Dear God, thank You for the Bible. Help us to memorize Your Word and to hide it in our hearts. Amen.

November 22

Do it!

Sharing Jesus with someone who doesn't know Him is offering someone the best gift ever! Have you ever told someone about Jesus?

Just like the disciples, we can be bold to share God's love with others in a kind and truthful way. We can bring support, encouragement, and a listening ear to those who may be struggling in their lives without Him.

Think of a few people in your life who don't know Jesus yet. Write their names on a postcard and set it in a place you will see every day. Pray that Jesus will reveal Himself to them and meet them at their point of need. Be a good friend to them and perhaps invite them to church or let them know what you are learning from this devotional. Be honest and bold in your faith and loving and gentle in your actions.

Dear God, help us love others well, especially if they don't know You yet. Be with us as we bless and serve others. Amen.

November 23

Talk About It

Sharing Jesus with others is one of the best ways to spend your time! We can learn more about Jesus through prayer and reading the Scriptures, and then we can share that Good News with others. What are some of your favorite ways to tell people about the love of Jesus?

Make a list of several small things you can do over the next week to share the love of Christ with someone who needs it. Pray for those in need, donate some old clothes to a homeless shelter, make a widow some cookies, hug your brother or sister, visit an elderly person, or walk a dog who could use a little exercise. Make acts like these a regular part of normal life this year and in the years to come. The small things in life can mean the most to someone who simply needs to know Jesus loves them. By discussing with your family some simple ways to share Christ's love, you can be prepared to serve when needed.

Dear God, show us how to share the Good News in loving and simple ways. Let us love others in the way You love us. Amen.

November 24

Serve One Another

The Good News can be shared in many different ways. Many times, the best way to share your faith is by using your gifts and talents in ways that honor God.

If you like to write, then consider writing a faith-based story to share with friends. If you like to play sports, perhaps point up to heaven when you or a teammate score a goal. This shows others that you give God credit for your successes. If you eat in the lunch cafeteria, you can bow your head and say a quick prayer before you eat. This honors God by blessing your food, and it shows others that you are thankful.

Thanking God and giving Him honor throughout our days, will allow others see our love for Jesus. They may decide to find out who He is!

Dear God, thank You for giving me gifts and talents that I enjoy. Help me to use those gifts and talents to share about You with others. Amen.

November 25

Eat Together

Making warm muffins is a wonderful way to start the day with your family. Enjoy baking a warm batch of pumpkin muffins together while talking through this week's lesson on Jesus' instructions to us to tell the world about Him!

You'll need:
1 (15 ounce) can pumpkin puree
¾ cup granulated sugar
½ cup vegetable oil
2 large eggs
1 tsp pumpkin pie spice
1 tsp baking soda
1 tsp vanilla extract
½ tsp kosher salt
1 ¾ cups all-purpose flour
Cupcake liners or baking spray

Pre-heat the oven to 375 degrees. Line your muffin tins or spray them with oil. Whisk all the ingredients except flour together in a large bowl. Combine until smooth. Fold the flour in with a spatula until everything is mixed. Make sure there are no large lumps. Fill the muffin tin and bake for 15 minutes. Rotate the pan and bake for 10–15 additional minutes, or until golden brown. Let your muffins cool for 5 minutes.

You may want to save some to share with a friend while you tell them about Jesus and all He's done for us.

Dear God, thank goodness for the Good News! Help us to celebrate You and honor You in everything we say and do. Amen.

November 26

Jesus Goes to Heaven
Luke 24; Acts 1

Forty days after Jesus rose from the dead, it was time for Jesus to return to Heaven. He gathered His disciples to share a few instructions. He told them to go into the world and share about Him; then He prayed for them. He told them to stay in Jerusalem and wait for Him to send them the Holy Spirit who would help them remember His words and give them power to tell the world about Him. He blessed His friends, and then He began to lift into the sky.

All the disciples watched Jesus ascend until they could no longer see Him. Two men in bright white appeared while they watched and asked them why they were looking at the sky. The men told them that Jesus would one day return in the same way He left.

They all praised God as they talked about and remembered their time with Jesus. They headed for Jerusalem to wait for the Holy Spirit, the Helper, just as Jesus instructed.

Dear God, thank You for defeating death, rising from the dead, and returning to Heaven. We will share Your mission until You come back again. Amen.

A Simple Prayer

This month, we are learning about gratitude.

We have learned that Jesus died, rose again, came back to visit His friends, and then ascended to Heaven. He gave His disciples important instructions to share His mission with the world, and He promised to send the Holy Spirit as the Helper—helping them tell others of Jesus' amazing gift of new life. We can be grateful to Jesus for our new lives and the honor of telling others about Him.

During November, pray this simple prayer with your family, expressing gratitude for all God has done for you.

Jesus, we are so grateful for You! Thank You for filling our hearts and inviting us into Your presence. Teach us how to cultivate gratitude in our lives and in our relationships with one another. Help us to grow and serve you always. Amen.

Bible Verse of the Week

"Why do you stand here looking into the sky? This same Jesus, who has been taken from you into heaven, will come back in the same way you have seen him go into heaven" (Acts 1:11; NIV).

One of the best ways to grow personally and as a family is to memorize Scripture.

This week in our reading, we learned Jesus ascended back into Heaven after giving His disciples instructions to share His Good News with the world.

Take the time to memorize Acts 1:11 with your family! Write it out and post it to your refrigerator. Let each person in your family have the opportunity to say it aloud, and then say it all together. Have fun enjoying the Word of God as a family!

Dear God, thank You for the Bible. Help us to memorize Your Word and to hide it in our hearts. Amen.

November 29

Do it!

This week, we read about Jesus when He ascended into Heaven. Can you imagine what it was like to watch Jesus rise into the sky? It was probably something amazing to see!

You likely have some dolls, toys, blocks, or markers around your house. Use those items to recreate the scene with Jesus and His disciples. Be creative. You can draw a picture or use items to represent Jesus and His followers. As you create, talk with your family about what it would have been like to be there. What do you think the disciples did while Jesus was lifting into the sky? Were they crying, celebrating, or raising their hands in worship? What would you do if you saw your best friend start to drift upward?

Enjoy sharing your thoughts as you create your ascension scene. Share some other astounding miracles of God as you work.

Dear God, Your ways are miraculous and Your love is so thoughtful. Help us to experience Your wonder as we learn about Your ways. Amen.

Talk About It

Jesus' rise into Heaven was a miraculous and wondrous event. Just as He always had, His manner of leaving Earth showed His disciples the beauty of being in connection with His Father. Before He left, Jesus gave the disciples very important instructions. He said to wait for the Holy Spirit who would help them tell the whole world about new life in Jesus.

Immediately, they were praising and worshipping Jesus. But after He was gone, they needed to follow through with His instructions. Jesus said He would come back someday, but until then, all His disciples have a lot to do.

Being prepared for His return means walking out His ministry in the ways He did when He was on Earth. It may seem like a big task to follow in the footsteps of Jesus, and it is! What are some of the things you could be doing while we wait for Jesus to come back? Talk about some ideas with your family, then do some of them today!

Dear God, we need Your help to live like You. Show us simple ways to honor You and tell others about you every day. Amen.

December 1

Serve One Another

Jesus served others throughout His life on Earth. We can serve each other in many of the same ways. What were some small steps to live like Jesus that you and your family discussed yesterday? Did you follow through with any of them yet?

If so, great! If not, try today. You can write down a few of the ideas you talked about, and post your list on the refrigerator. After you do each one, simply cross it off. Sometimes we need a little help to remember to do good, and that's ok! By being intentional about working to serve one another, it will become a regular part of our days.

You can always ask the Helper to be with you and help you remember to serve. He loves to lead you to great ideas and people who need Him.

Dear God, help me to remember to serve others. Send your Holy Spirit to guide me as I uplift the people around me. Amen.

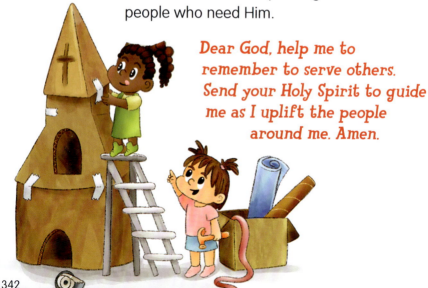

Eat Together

Jesus rose up into Heaven. There are many foods to bake that "rise," but in a much different way.

Have you ever heard of yeast, baking soda, or baking powder? These are called leavening agents; they cause dough to expand . . . or rise.

Take on the family mission today to find a simple recipe that includes a leavening agent. Pay close attention to the dish before you put it in the oven and after you get it out. You might even want to take a picture to really realize the difference.

During the baking or rising process, share what you learned this week with your family. What about Jesus' ascension was the most surprising to you? What did you learn about Jesus? What did you learn about His disciples and the ways they followed Jesus' instructions?

Celebrate Jesus today and enjoy your newly-risen treat!

Dear God, help us to receive the fullness of Your life. We are so grateful that we get to participate in Your mission. Amen.

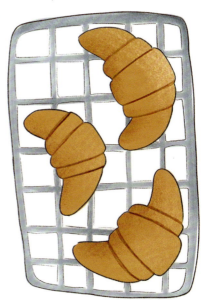

December 3
The Disciples Spread the Word
Acts 2-3, 9, 12, 16

Jesus' followers had gone to Jerusalem as Jesus instructed. One day during a religious holiday when Jerusalem was full of visitors, the believers were praying together. Suddenly, a wind came from Heaven and whirled through the room. Right away, the believers became filled with the Holy Spirit, and they started to praise God in all sorts of different languages. The people outside heard the noise and wondered what was happening.

Peter went outside and suddenly became a very bold and effective speaker and able to make himself heard over the thousands of people who had gathered. By the time Peter finished sharing, three thousand people had become Christians and were baptized. After this, the disciples went out and performed more miracles and good acts in the name of Jesus.

During this time, a man named Saul was persecuting Christians. This continued until he was traveling to another city called Damascus; he was suddenly confronted by Jesus! In an instant, Saul was blinded. He continued to Damascus where the Lord sent a man named Ananias to pray for him and his sight was restored. Saul's name was changed to Paul, and he went on to preach and suffer for Jesus, just as Peter and the other disciples did.

Dear God, thank You for sending the Holy Spirit to help us. Give us strength to be bold and have courage like Paul and the disciples. Amen.

A Simple Prayer

This month, we are learning about generosity. God showed His fullness to the disciples this week by sending the Holy Spirit to help them after Jesus ascended to Heaven. By experiencing the Father, Son, and Holy Spirit, we are enabled to be generous to others in miraculous ways. Peter and the disciples went out boldly to proclaim the Good News of Jesus; we can do the same.

During December, pray this simple prayer with your family, expressing thankfulness for God's generosity toward you.

Jesus, You are the giver of life! Thank You for being born into this world, dying on the cross, and coming back to life in resurrection power. Teach us how to cultivate generosity in our lives and in our relationships with one another. Help us to generously share You, always. Amen.

December 5

Bible Verse of the Week

"Peter replied, Repent and be baptized, every one of you, in the name of Jesus Christ for the forgiveness of your sins'" (Acts 2:38; NIV).

One of the best ways to grow personally and as a family is to memorize Scripture.

This week in our reading, the Holy Spirit came like a mighty wind to fill the people of God. The Holy Spirit made them bold and courageous in sharing their faith.

Take the time to memorize Acts 2:38 with your family! Write it out and post it to your refrigerator. Let each person in your family have the opportunity to say it aloud, and then say it all together. Have fun enjoying the Word of God as a family!

Dear God, Thank You for the Bible. Help us to memorize Your Word and to hide it in our hearts. Amen.

December 6

Do it!

The Holy Spirit is the Helper! There is evidence and instruction all through the Scriptures to learn about Him and walk in step with Him.

Grab your Bible and open it to the Book of John. Together with your family, read chapters 14, 15, and 16. As you do, ask God to show you new things about the Holy Spirit.

Have each person make a list of some of the different ways that Jesus said the Holy Spirit would help us. What sticks out to you the most? Is there anything that brings you comfort or joy? Does anything convict you? God fills us with His Spirit who encourages us, corrects us, and comforts us. We can see the Holy Spirit in action throughout Scripture.

Spend time today thanking God for His Helper, the Holy Spirit, and be encouraged in His love for you.

Dear God, You are so good to us. Thank You for sending the Helper to bring us into a better understanding of Your love and sacrifice for us. Amen.

December 7

Talk About It

Peter was suddenly filled with boldness and courage to preach about Jesus. Many people were saved and baptized as a result. Peter was able to speak with power and clarity because the Helper was there within Him.

Just as Jesus said, the Holy Spirit was sent to give the disciples the boldness they needed to share about Jesus and to stand strong in the face of persecution and death. Many of the disciples were beaten, mocked, put in jail, or killed because of their courage and faith in Jesus. They needed the Holy Spirit to be with them because they had a very big job to do.

Have you ever shared Jesus with someone? Did that person respond well? Was it a difficult conversation? Telling others about God can be complicated at times because people come from many different backgrounds, sometimes they suffer from difficult circumstances or life experiences. Some people might not want you to share about Jesus. These are some of the very reasons Jesus sent help. Even when sharing your faith is tough, you can be sure that God loves you and is with you.

Dear God, help me to be bold, wise, and kind when I share about You. Lead me to people who are ready to hear about all You have done for them. Amen.

December 8

Serve One Another

The Book of Acts tells how the people of God served and shared with one another. The believers gathered together often to eat and pray. If someone in the community was in need, others would sell what they had in order to provide for that need. They lived life in harmony with one another as they learned about the goodness of God.

Living in loving harmony with the people around us is wonderful! God wants us to love our families and love the family of God. What are a few ways you can serve your family today and throughout this season?

Christmas is coming quickly. Can you think of any handcrafted gifts you could make for each of your family members? You might draw a picture, or create a craft of some kind. You could bake someone's favorite cookies or give coupons for housework. You could even write each family member an encouraging note to tell them all the things you love about them.

No matter what you choose, spend today planning ways to serve your family, just like the people in Acts.

Dear God, thank You for creating family. Help us to love one another well and to share with each other. Amen.

Eat Together

The church in Acts spent a lot of time gathered around a table, eating and telling stories. They loved to hear from each other about what God was doing in each of their lives while celebrating Him. You can do the same!

Take it easy today, and order a pizza from your favorite, local restaurant. Notice how the pizza is cut into several different pieces. Every person gets a piece (or two) of the larger whole, and that can remind you of the church in Acts—everyone got whatever they needed.

While enjoying your pizza, take some time to share about what the Helper has taught you this week. Listen to your family members without interrupting and just enjoy hearing from one another. Celebrate each story and thank God for a full belly!

Dear God, You are so generous with us. Thank You for helping us, guiding us, and providing for us. We love You. Amen.

December 10
John Sees Heaven
Revelation 1, 4, 21

John spent his life sharing the love of Jesus. He was exiled to the Island of Patmos because of the persecution of Christians. While John was celebrating Sabbath, he heard a voice sounding like a trumpet. That voice instructed John to write what he was about to hear and see.

John looked and saw a man standing in between seven lampstands. The man was very white like snow, from the top of his head and through his hair. His eyes were blazing, and his feet were like bronze. His voice was like rushing water, and his face shone like the glory of God. John fell face down in reverence and awe.

The man told him not to be afraid. He said that He was the beginning and the end; the One who was dead and but now forever alive. John went with Him to heaven where he saw rainbows and jewels. There was a throne; around it were elders wearing robes and crowns continually worshipping. John saw a new heaven and a new earth, and he also saw the New Jerusalem. The One who was sitting on the throne said, "I am making everything new." The city was so bright with the glory of God that it didn't even need a sun or moon. The names of the people who lived there were written in a book by God called The Book of Life.

Dear God, heaven is such a treasure! Thank You for showing us glimpses of it in Your Word. Give us the grace to understand what You describe it to be. Amen.

December 11

A Simple Prayer

This month, we are learning about generosity. God was generous to John when He showed him how heaven looked and felt. Even though John was exiled and alone, God was with him. How amazing it must have been for him to see the beauty of God's dwelling place and His throne.

During December, pray this simple prayer with your family, expressing thankfulness for God's generosity toward you.

Jesus, You are the giver of life! Thank You for being born into this world, dying on the cross, and coming back to life in resurrection power. Teach us how to cultivate generosity in our lives and in our relationships with one another. Help us to generously share You, always. Amen.

December 12

Bible Verse of the Week

"The One who was sitting on the throne said, 'Look! I am making everything new!'" (Revelation 21:5; NCV).

One of the best ways to grow personally and as a family is to memorize Scripture.

This week in our reading, we discovered that John was taken to heaven to see rainbows, jewels, the throne, and more. He was given the special opportunity to see things no one else had ever seen and to write it all down.

Take the time to memorize Revelation 21:5 with your family! Write it out and post it to your refrigerator. Let each person in your family have the opportunity to say it aloud, and then say it all together. Have fun enjoying the Word of God as a family!

Dear God, thank You for the Bible. Help us to memorize Your Word and to hide it in our hearts. Amen.

December 13
Do it!

Revelation is full of descriptions of Heaven. When John was taken to Heaven, he experienced a man with bright white hair and eyes of fire. His feet were glowing, and His voice sounded like rushing water. John saw an incredible rainbow and colorful jewels. There was a glorious throne and elders worshipping the One seated on the throne. It was a lot to take in!

Take time today for the members of your family to read through Revelation 1, 4, and 21. Take turns reading it aloud to one another and try to imagine what John saw. Grab a set of crayons or markers, and draw the awesome sights as you imagine them.

Share your pictures with one another and talk about what it might be like to see Heaven for yourself. Spend time talking with your family about the things from Revelation you chose to draw. What most interested you? Did anything surprise you? Talk about what it might be like when you see it for yourself!

Dear God, You made Heaven beautiful! Thank You for sharing some of the details with us. Help us to live in awe of You. Amen.

December 14

Talk About It

Seeing Heaven was a miraculous gift for John. He was told to write down everything he saw. Aren't you grateful that you can read the details? Revelation is full of information that may seem so different than everyday life on Earth. It gives a glimpse of what to expect when Christians get to Heaven.

Over the last year, we have looked at Scripture from Genesis to Revelation. Throughout, the Bible makes it clear that Jesus is the Way, the Truth, and the Life. He is the Savior who died for His people, came back to life, and then went to Heaven to prepare a place for Christians to live for eternity.

As a family, you have read through many of the most well-known stories of the Bible and have had the opportunity to learn about God's plan for His people. As you read about John's experience in Heaven, you get a first-hand glimpse of the goodness God has planned for you!

What is your favorite part of John's story? Talk about it with your family and enjoy discussing this special look at heaven.

Dear God, thank You for saving us. You are the Way, the Truth, and the Life. We are eager to see Heaven, and spend eternity with you! Amen.

December 15

Serve One Another

John lived in a time when Christians were severely persecuted. He was exiled to the island of Patmos because he would not stop preaching the Gospel of Jesus. While on the island, John continued worshiping God and was practicing his Sabbath day of rest when he was given this divine revelation.

What does John's experience reveal about God's provision, even in the middle of persecution or punishment? John had done nothing wrong in the eyes of God. Those in power did not want him to share about Jesus, but John obeyed God. God provided for him because he had been punished for doing the right thing.

This is a good reminder to keep serving Jesus, whether in obvious ways or in quiet ones, knowing that God is generous with us as we walk with Him. We can show Jesus to one another no matter the circumstance, knowing He will provide for us. Be kind to one another today; tell the truth gently, serve with joy, and share the Good News in all the little things you do.

Dear God, You are our provider. Help us serve You and honor You, knowing You will always be with us. Amen.

Eat Together

If you were stranded on a tropical island, what fruits do you think you would find? Most likely, you'd find coconuts, pineapples, bananas, or papayas. You might even find avocado, guava, mango, or starfruit.

Head to your grocery store as a family and browse the produce aisle. See what tropical fruits they have in stock and consider trying something new. If you can't find something that suits you, you might want to grab a pre-made smoothie in the refrigerator section or head to the freeze-dried fruit and find one that contains a tropical delight.

As a family, enjoy your fresh fruit, smoothie, or other find. Talk about what you learned this week by reading John's experience on the island. Celebrate the fact that God shows up and provides for us, just like He did for John!

Dear God, thank You for sending us the help we need. Please motivate us to search out and learn more about what Scripture reveals regarding Heaven and what is to come. Amen.

December 17
The Old Testament

By now, your family has made it through the most common stories of the Bible. Congratulations! The Scriptures are divided into two major sections, the Old Testament and the New Testament. The Old Testament contains the writings of men who lived before Jesus was born, and the New Testament contains writings from approximately nine men who lived during the nearly 100 years after Jesus came into the world.

If you followed this devotional in order, you covered the Old Testament portion in the first half of this book, ending on Week 25. In Scripture, the Old Testament contains thirty-nine books and shares about the Jewish people, their history, and the promise of a coming Messiah.

In the Old Testament, you can read stories about Adam and Eve, Noah, Moses, David, Daniel, and many more. By studying this part of Scripture, you learned a lot about the history of God's people and His faithfulness to them. Take a minute to thank God for all He taught you through the Old Testament.

Dear God, thank You for sharing Your story with us. Thank You for inspiring men to write of Your love and actions from the beginning of time. Amen.

December 18

A Simple Prayer

This month, we are learning about generosity.

God was so generous to His people throughout the Old Testament. We learned about His faithfulness, even though they failed to follow Him over and over again. God loves to guide His people and correct them, when needed. He is the perfect Father, training us to live in the best ways. He knew we would need Jesus to help us; the prophets of the Old Testament foretold His coming to provide hope for God's people.

During December, pray this simple prayer with your family, expressing generosity for all God has done for you.

Jesus, You are the giver of life! Thank You for being born into this world, dying on the cross, and coming back to life in resurrection power. Teach us how to cultivate generosity in our lives and in our relationships with one another. Help us to generously share You, always. Amen.

December 19

Bible Verse of the Week

"God saw all that he had made, and it was very good" (Genesis 1:31; NIV).

One of the best ways to grow personally and as a family is to memorize Scripture.

Go back to the very first story in this devotional called *The Very Beginning*. Look up the Scripture you memorized that week. Do you remember it?

Take the time to review Genesis 1:31 with your family! Write it out and post it to your refrigerator. Let each person in your family have the opportunity to say it aloud, and then say it all together. Have fun enjoying the Word of God as a family!

Dear God, thank You for the Bible. Help us to memorize Your Word and to hide it in our hearts. Amen.

December 20

Do it!

The Old Testament contains many stories about the history of the world and its kings and prophets. It also presents the future promise of Jesus. Along with your family, look through the first half of the Table of Contents for this devotional. Write down three or four of the stories that had the biggest impact on you. Glance through the pages of what you learned that week, what activity you did, and what prayers you prayed.

As you do, take time as a family to thank God for what He taught you. Go to the Scriptures and re-read the stories in full and savor the words on the pages. Each time you read your Bible, you can learn something new! No matter how many times you read it, the Word is living and active (Hebrews 4:12). You can read the Bible over and over again and always receive something fresh.

Enjoy refreshing your mind through what you learned this year. Celebrate, and keep on learning!

Dear God, Your word is living and active, and You have a lot to teach us. Help us to read and re-read the Bible, soaking in Your Word each day. Amen.

Talk About It

By looking through all stories you read during the first half of this year, you will realize how much of the Old Testament you've learned. Though the Old Testament can sometimes feel very big and intimidating, God made sure to break it down in just the right way so people can learn about Him. At times, it's important to dig deeper into stories that inspire you.

Out of the three or four stories you chose to write down yesterday, which one is your favorite? Sit with your family and share your favorite Old Testament Bible story; then listen to theirs. Have a conversation about how the stories were significant to each of you and why. What did you learn? And how does what you learned inspire you to live differently?

After you have spent time sharing with one another, take a few minutes to pray and thank God for what He is teaching each of you.

Dear God, thank You for teaching us through the Old Testament! Help us as we are encouraged, inspired, and learning to understand what You have said in Your Word. Amen.

December 22

Serve One Another

After you have reviewed all you learned this year in the Old Testament, write down a few of your favorite stories, and then share those stories with your family. Next, take the opportunity to share the Bible outside of the house!

Who would really like to hear the stories you have to share? Do you have any friends who love to read or love stories? Share with them the lessons that impacted you, and encourage them to read them for themselves. By sharing what you have learned with those around you, you bless them with the love and encouragement Jesus placed within you. They may even be led to find the source of that love and encouragement—Jesus!

Take a few minutes today and think of friends or family you can go see or call on the phone to tell them about Jesus. You can even write a letter or an email to someone you love. No matter who you choose to contact, you can smile and know that God loves sharing Himself with you and your friends.

Dear God, please lead me to someone who would love to hear Your stories and listen to Your Word. Be with me as I share what has meant a lot to me. Amen.

Eat Together

As you and your family have read through the Old Testament, you have had many snacks together. Some have been quite simple, while others may have required a trip to the grocery store. A few required light cooking, but all of them were tasty.

You've chosen your favorite stories from the Old Testament, now you can choose a few of your favorite recipes! From charcuterie boards to apples, from chili to hot dogs, salsa to Jello™, there are so many foods we've shared with our families so far. As a family, find a recipe from this devotional that you would like to enjoy again.

While eating that snack, review the story focus of that week. Remind yourselves of what you learned from reading together, praying together, and serving one another. As always, thank God for what you learned, and share it with someone else!

Dear God, You are so generous, so loving, so forgiving. Thank You for all the grace you give to us each day as we live and grow in You. Amen.

December 24

The New Testament

Your year spent in The Bible For Me devotional is nearly over. You and your family have made it through the most common stories of the Bible. This is quite an accomplishment!

You will recall that the Scriptures are divided into two major sections: the Old Testament and the New Testament. The Old Testament contains the writings before Jesus was born, and the New Testament shares the writings from the events surrounding His birth onward.

If you followed this devotional in order, you made it through the New Testament stories in the second half of this book, starting with Week 26 and ending with Week 50. The New Testament contains twenty-seven books and shares about the life, death, resurrection, works, and teachings of Jesus.

The stories you read about Jesus, His disciples and all the lives they touched are contained in the New Testament. By studying this part of Scripture, you learned a lot about God's story and His faithfulness to us through the Savior, Jesus. Take a minute to thank God for all He taught you through the New Testament.

Dear God, thank You for sharing Your life with us. Help us to appreciate and continue to learn from the stories we hear about You. Amen.

A Simple Prayer

This month, we are learning about generosity. God was so generous to His people throughout the New Testament because He sent Jesus to the world. We learned about the life of Jesus, all the miracles He did, and His death and resurrection. Jesus loves to be with His people and teach them the ways of His Father. He knew we would need the Holy Spirit to help us, and the New Testament teaches us a lot about Him.

This December, pray this simple prayer with your family, expressing generosity for all God has done for you.

Jesus, You are the giver of life! Thank You for being born into this world, dying on the cross, and coming back to life in resurrection power. Teach us how to cultivate generosity in our lives and in our relationships with one another. Help us to generously share You, always. Amen.

Bible Verse of the Week

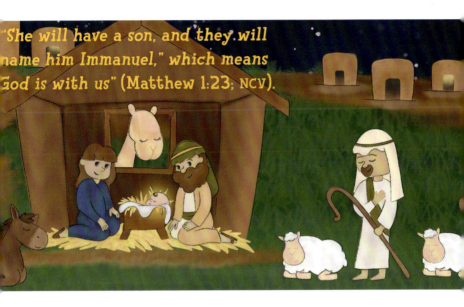

"She will have a son, and they will name him Immanuel," which means 'God is with us'" (Matthew 1:23; NCV).

One of the best ways to grow personally and as a family is to memorize Scripture.

Go back to Week 27 in this devotional entitled God With Us. Look up the Scripture you memorized that week. Do you remember it?

Take the time to review Matthew 1:23 with your family! Write it out and post it to your refrigerator. Let each person in your family have the opportunity to say it aloud, and then say it all together. Have fun enjoying the Word of God as a family!

Dear God, thank You for the Bible. Help us to memorize Your Word and to hide it in our hearts. Amen.

December 27
Do it!

The New Testament contains many stories about the birth of Jesus, His life on Earth filled with miracles and teachings, His death on the cross, and His resurrection. It also shares much about the lives of His followers after Jesus went back to Heaven.

Look through the second half of the Table of Contents for this devotional. Write down three or four of the stories that had the biggest impact on you. Glance through the pages of what you learned that week, what activity you did, and what prayers you prayed.

As you do, thank God for what He taught and showed you. Go to the Scriptures and re-read the stories in full and savor the words on the pages. Each time you read your Bible, you can learn something new! No matter how many times you read it, the Word is living and active (Hebrews 4:12). You can read the Bible over and over again and always learn something fresh.

Enjoy refreshing your mind through what you learned this year. Celebrate, and keep on learning!

Dear God, Your word is living and active, and You have a lot to teach us. Help us to read and re-read the Bible, soaking in the Word each day. Amen.

Talk About It

As you look through all the pages and stories you read during the second half of this year, you will realize you experienced quite a bit of the New Testament. The New Testament is the perfect way to learn about the life of Jesus and how the Holy Spirit now works in Christians. It's important to dig deeper into the teachings of Jesus that inspire you. There are always more amazing things to learn!

Out of the three or four stories you chose to write down yesterday, which one is your favorite? Take time to sit with your family today while each of you shares a favorite New Testament Bible story. Have a conversation about how the story was significant to you and why. What did it teach you? How does it inspire you to live differently?

After you have spent time sharing with one another, take a few minutes to pray and thank God for what He is teaching each of you.

Dear God, thank You for teaching us about the New Testament! Help us be encouraged and inspired as we seek to understand what You had said and done. Amen.

December 29

Serve One Another

You have reviewed all you learned this year in the New Testament, wrote down a few of your favorite stories, and shared those stories with your family. Now, it's time to take the Bible outside the house!

Who would really like to hear the stories you have to share? Do you have any friends who love to read or love stories? Share with them the lessons that impacted you and encourage them to read them for themselves. By sharing what you have learned with those around you, you bless them with the love and encouragement Jesus placed within you. They may even be led to find the source of that love and encouragement—Jesus!

Take a few minutes today and think of friends or family you can go see or call on the phone to tell them about Jesus. You can even write a letter or an email to someone you love. No matter who you choose to contact, you can smile and know that God loves sharing Himself with you and your friends.

Dear God, please lead me to someone who would love to hear Your stories and listen to Your Word. Be with me as I share all I have learned. Amen.

December 30

Eat Together

You and your family have enjoyed many snacks together as you read through the New Testament. Some have been quite simple, while others may have required a trip to the grocery store. A few required light cooking, but all of them were tasty.

You've chosen your favorite stories from the New Testament, now you can choose a few of your favorite recipes! The snacks have ranged from burgers to angel food cake, trail mix to pizza boats, comfort foods to warm beverages, as well as many other fun foods. Have each person in your family find a recipe they would like to repeat and then all of you can enjoy them again.

While eating your snack, review the story focus from the week where you found this suggested food. Remind yourselves of all you learned that week as you read together, prayed together, and served one another. As always, thank God for what you learned, and share it with someone else!

Dear God, You are so generous, so loving, so forgiving. Thank You for all the grace you give to us each day as we live and grow in You. Amen.

December 31

Conclusion

It's official! You have spent 365 days reading the Bible, praying, learning, sharing, serving, and eating together as a family. As you have made your way through these stories and lessons from Scripture, you have established rhythms for your family that will last a lifetime.

By focusing on and completing each one of these devotionals and activities, you have spent your time in a way that honors God and nourishes your soul. Spend this last day together sharing your favorite parts of the journey, whether it be family time, memorizing Scripture, serving others, or cooking snacks together. As you do, thank God for what He has done in your midst, and be encouraged to continue your family devotions so your family can thrive.

Be blessed as you live out the joy of Jesus in you!

Dear God, thank You for time together as a family. Help us to keep reading the Scriptures and learning about You every day. Amen.

What We Learned

Now that you've finished this devotional as a family, take time to go back and review favorite times of learning together. Use these next pages to remember and thank God for all He has taught you.